TALES ALONG

THE KING'S HIGHWAY

of
South Carolina

Tales along the King's Highway
of South Carolina

Blanche W. Floyd

Winston-Salem, North Carolina

Library of Congress Catalog Card Number 99-72996

ISBN 1-878177-10-9

Bandit Books, Inc.

P.O. Box 11721

Winston-Salem, NC 27116-1721

(336) 785-7417

Distributed by John F. Blair, Publisher

(800) 222-9796

Cover illustration by Ruth Chestnut Cox

Cover design by Molly Yarbrough

For J. K.
my husband and helper
and for our children
Kirk, Joyce, and Beth
who love the Grand Strand
as we do

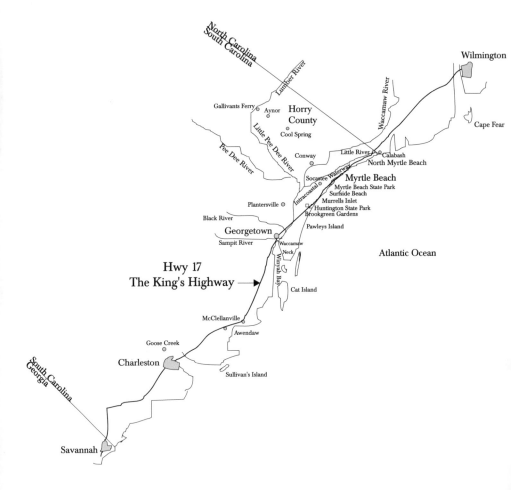

Wilmington

North Carolina
South Carolina

Lumber River

Gallivants Ferry

Aynor

Horry
County

Cool Spring

Waccamaw River

Cape Fear

Little Pee Dee River

Pee Dee River

Conway

Little River
Calabash
North Myrtle Beach

Socastee
Myrtle Beach

Intracoastal Waterway

Myrtle Beach State Park
Surfside Beach
Murrells Inlet
Huntington State Park
Brookgreen Gardens

Plantersville

Black River

Georgetown

Sampit River

Pawleys Island

Waccamaw
Neck

Atlantic Ocean

Hwy 17
The King's Highway ➤

Winyah Bay

Cat Island

McClellanville

Awendaw

Goose Creek

Charleston

Sullivan's Island

South Carolina
Georgia

Savannah

TABLE OF CONTENTS

Acknowledgments

Introduction - The King's Highway   1

1   The Legend of the Sewee Indians   3

2   Anne Bonney, Woman Pirate   7

3   Stede Bonnet, The Gentleman Pirate   13

4   Georgetown, Historic Seaport   19

5   The Independent Republic of Horry   27

6   Plantations   33

7   Indigo Blue   39

8   Hopsewee Plantation   43

9   Peachtree Manor   47

10   Hampton Plantation   49

11   The Ghost of John Henry

         at Hampton Plantation   55

12   Pawleys Island   61

13   The South Carolina State Flag   65

14   The Bartram Trail   69

15 Florena Budwin, The Captain's Orderly   73

16 Coming Home in 1865   79

17 The Ghosts of Old Gunn Church   85

18 Sandy Island, A Place Called Home   89

19 The Dutchman of Medway Plantation   93

20 The Haunting of Litchfield Manor   97

21 Presidential Visitors   101

22 The Old Arke   109

23 A Whale of a Tale   113

24 The First Pavilion at Myrtle Beach   117

25 Proper Beach Attire   121

26 Beware the Riptide   129

27 Hobcaw Barony   133

28 Baker John   139

29 Myrtle Beach Air Force Base   145

30 A Season of Storms   151

31 Ghosts of the Coast   157

32 The Witch's Curse   161

ACKNOWLEDGMENTS

My sincere thanks to everyone who helped me in the collection and telling of these tales. So often a shared memory or a forgotten picture brings about an interesting story.

For example, Rena Mae Bellamy told me that her parents took their horse and buggy to Pine Island, after their wedding in Socastee. From Pine Island, they rode the train to Conway and stayed in the old Kingston Hotel for a wonderful honeymoon trip. What a nice memory!

The Nance sisters told me about the first school at Myrtle Beach and the one their mother attended on Pine Island Road. One of the hazards of walking to school was the possibility of meeting bears on the way. The Nance sisters also described the Junior-Senior reception held in the dining room of the Lafayette Manor in the 1930s. They shared memories of World War II and the ever-present threat of enemy submarines lurking along the beaches.

Rudy Benik, now deceased, was one of the first soldiers at the air base in 1942. He remembered the primitive huts and unheated buildings the men lived in, a step up from tents.

Marcus Smith spent summers at the beach from the 1920s, and moved to the beach in the 1940s. He shared many helpful ideas and memories of earlier days, especially about the telephones and the pavilions.

Such information isn't found in reference books. It comes from the hearts and minds of friends who share. My sincere thanks to these folks and others who helped.

As always, the staff at Chapin Memorial Library went the extra mile by helping confirm dates and quotations, by phoning Greenville for information about the Cuban Missile Crisis, by going through the writings of Sir Walter Scott to find a name. Perhaps these aren't earthshaking historical facts, but they were important to this writer. To list all the staff's help would take many pages.

My thanks to family members, who were always helpful and supportive. My husband J. K. continues to be my driver, photographer, and helper in every way. He proofreads and finds my mistakes.

Finally thanks to my editor and his staff for their helpfulness, and to Stewart Pabst and the Horry County Museum for their resources and timely assistance.

INTRODUCTION

The King's Highway

Tales of pirates and ghosts
Along our Carolina Coast
And of settlers who came to stay.

A song heard along the beach recently has these words: "We're walking on the King's Highway!" The song has no connection to Highway 17, but it brings to mind the centuries-old name for the Coastal Highway. From earliest Colonial days in the 1600s the road was known as the King's Highway, and the name is still used today.

The road began as an Indian path. Later the kings of England sent couriers along the path to carry important messages through the colonies. These were usually edicts or tax laws. The proud and independent farmers along the King's Highway in South Carolina paid little attention to such laws. They had wrested a living and survived in the wilderness; they took care of themselves and their neighbors. Their stretch of the King's Highway ran across the Waccamaw River, through deep swamps, and impenetrable thickets.

Many have traveled the Highway: the young Marquis de Lafayette of France, Baron de Kalb of Prussia, Reverend George Whitfield, Bishop Francis Asbury, George Washington and other United States presidents, poor settlers, rich planters, pirates, traders, and fugitives. The stories of some of these travelers and the places they visited make up the tales of this book. From ancient times until today, each person or group had a story to tell. From those stories, history unfolds.

No state has a more varied or colorful history than South Carolina. The Palmetto state has always struggled with good times and bad, peace and war, victory and defeat. Out of these challenges has emerged a resilient population, ready to face problems, and often achieve greatness.

In earlier times, those who passed along the King's Highway saw unusual flora and fauna. Cedars, pines, and yaupon trees grew just back of high sand dunes, which had been sculpted by ocean winds and tides. Most of these are gone now. They have been replaced by high-rise buildings, manicured lawns, and spectacular shrubbery, right down to the high tide mark. Still, new tales develop or old ones continue.

Let's explore the King's Highway together.

1

THE LEGEND OF
THE SEWEE INDIANS

Have you ever seen a ghostly fire on the beach, burning desperately against wind and spray as a signal for eyes that will never see it?

Perhaps you've caught a glimpse of the ghosts of the grieving Sewee Indians.

*   *   *

For countless centuries the Sewee Indians and other tribes roamed the Coastal Plain. The "ee" ending for names was a characteristic of the Siouan Nation tribes: Sewee, Pee Dee, Wateree, Wampee, Socastee, and others. Languages were similar and the people lived simple lives, with plentiful game, fish, crabs, oysters, berries, wild grains, and roots for food. The Sewee village lay south of Winyah Bay (present-day Georgetown) between the Santee River and the beach.

In the seventeenth century English settlers began to move among the tribes. Traders brought items the Indians found hard to resist: bright beads and calico for the women, knives and tools for the men, and simple whistles and balls for the children. The Indians bought the cheap trinkets with rich furs and skins.

Soon the Indians figured out they were overpaying. When they asked for fairer prices in the 1690s, the traders replied they had to trade by the rules? Who made the rules? Why, of course the Great White Father, the King of England who lived across the water. If they wanted to change the rules, the Indians had to talk to the king.

The Indians believed the traders' lie.

The Sewee Tribal Council met and decided to prepare for the voyage across the water. If they built their biggest boats, visited the king, showed him their furs, and told him of their troubles with the traders, surely the Great White Father would understand and help them.

The men immediately set to work burning and scraping out cypress canoes, some of them twenty feet long. The task took long weeks, but the Sewees worked hard while keeping an eye on the far horizon where they would travel. When the canoes were finished, the tribe loaded them with furs and skins. Then the strongest and most capable men guided the canoes out into the ocean.

The women and children watched proudly and waved good-bye.

They would wait for the return of their men, which would be soon.

Night after night the women built a bonfire on top of a tall sand dune next to the broad beach. They piled on broken pieces of wood they had gathered so the flames would leap up into the darkness, a bright signal to guide the men home. Moons passed. The blue waters of the Atlantic stretched out to the horizon, but there was no sign of Indian canoes.

They realized they couldn't survive without the elders and braves. Who would hunt and fish to supply the food? Who would make the important decisions? Who would defend them if another tribe attacked?

Small children helped drag tree limbs, pine cones, and trash to the sand dune to feed the fire. Long months passed, but the tribe kept up the vigil. The men had sailed away so confidently. Surely they would return. As winter and hunger set in, the tribe's faith faded. The waiting group gradually grew smaller as women and children wandered off to join other tribes nearby.

Finally the night came when there was no fire on the beach.

The men never returned.

Unfortunately the men had left in the early fall, the season of storms. They had been at sea only a few days when a violent tropical storm struck, overturning the canoes and dumping men and cargo into the unforgiving Atlantic Ocean.

The History of South Carolina by Mary C. Simms-Oliphant states that a devastating hurricane occurred in 1699. Could this be the storm in the legend?

A few of the men clung to the overturned canoes long enough to be picked up by English ships. The sailors listened to the Indians' amazing story, then took them to the Caribbean and sold them as slaves.

The Sewee village lay deserted. The men hadn't returned to their beautiful Coastal Plain homeland. The women had had to save their children by taking them to other tribes. Drifting sand and falling leaves, blown by autumn winds and rain, eventually covered the village. Finally there was left no sign that the Sewee tribe had ever existed. They were almost forgotten, but not quite.

The women never forgot their lost men, and told their children and grandchildren the story. The legend has survived three centuries.

*   *   *

So if you see that ghostly fire on the beach, have pity on those who wait for loved ones to return.

2

ANNE BONNEY

WOMAN PIRATE

Anne Bonney went on trial for piracy in Jamaica in 1720. One man who witnessed the trial became an admirer of hers. He described her regal bearing, sparkling red hair, and "sea-water green eyes." This admirer had been a pirate himself, and had accepted a pardon from King George I of England in 1717. He acquired land near Charleston, and became a wealthy planter. Watching Anne Bonney at the trial, he fell in love and decided to take her back to Charleston and marry her.

Anne was born in County Cork, Ireland in the late 1600s. Her father was William Cormac, an Attorney-at-law, and her mother was his wife's maid. Cormac tried to adopt the little girl, and tried to dress her as a little boy relative, but his wife protested both times. So Cormac left Ireland and his wife, and took the maid and little Anne to the New World. They settled at Goose Creek, near Charleston. Cormac prospered as an attorney and planter, and bought more land along the Black River, close to George-town. After her mother died of typhoid fever, Anne kept house for her father. She disdained the pretentious social life of the day in Charleston, preferring life on the plantation.

Cormac adored his daughter and gave her every advantage. He planned for her to marry well and inherit all his wealth. Instead Anne fell in love with a penniless sailor she met on the Charleston waterfront named James Bonney. Knowing her father would never accept Bonney, they married secretly, hoping to force Cormac to bless the union. He refused. Furious and disappointed, he turned them both out "without a groat" (a four-pence coin).

All her life Anne was known for her "fierce and courageous temper," and for violent acts against servants. Her father always tried to control her wild streak, much to her resentment. Marriage to Bonney freed her from any control.

The couple drifted down to the Caribbean. Bonney wanted to settle in a house with his pretty wife, but that wasn't what Anne had in mind. She soon left Bonney for a handsome, rich, daredevil pirate, Captain Jack Rackam. Always donning fancy clothes and striped breeches, he was known as "Calico Jack."

It didn't take Anne long to persuade her pirate lover to let her go to sea with him. She disguised herself in men's clothing. The wild life at sea suited her perfectly, and she fought as fiercely as any man. According to Hugh F. Rankin's book on coastal pirates, Anne carried a dagger in her belt and used it in a cruel and bloodthirsty way. When the pirates boarded ships at sea, Anne showed no mercy to her helpless victims.

Her greatest delight was to attack ships near where she had

grown up with her father, along the South Carolina coast. She even encouraged other pirate captains to do the same. She knew the coast so well, she was able to guide the pirates into safe coves and inlets for hiding and counting their booty.

Men came and went on the ships due to injuries, deaths, ill feelings, or the decision to seek a pardon. One day a new pirate came on board, and Anne fell in love with him. However the pirate had a surprise for Anne—Mark Read turned out to be Mary Read. Disguised just like Anne, Mary had lived an equally exciting life, and the two became constant companions and confidants. Mary had served in the British army, disguised as a man, until she grew bored and ran away. The sea appealed to her and she ended up on a pirate ship.

The two women ended their charade, much to the surprise of Calico Jack's crew. They started wearing women's clothes. As the captain's favorite, Anne had special privileges, which she now demanded also for Mary. The women lorded these privileges over the other pirates. But when the lookout sighted a prize ship, the women slipped into men's trousers and jackets, and knotted kerchiefs around their heads to hide their long hair. Anne and Mary were cruel, boarding the ships with cutlass and marlinespike slashing. Blood flowed when they were around.

In October, 1720, Calico Jack decided to take the ship on a restful cruise in the islands. He ordered shore leave for the men. Possibly some crew members talked too much, for the governor of Jamaica heard the ship was there and sent out an armed sloop to capture it. In the battle, Anne and Mary fought like tigers, but the other pirates threw down their weapons and surrendered. The women taunted the men for being cowards, right through the trial.

The news went out that Captain Calico Jack Rackam had been captured. The prisoners were taken to St. Jago de la Vega, Jamaica to stand trial. Victims and former pirates showed up to watch.

Sketch by John D. Ellington
Courtesy of the N.C. Division of Archives and History

When the judge asked Anne Bonney and Mary Read how they would plead, both grinned and said, "My Lord, we Plead our Bellies." Since an unborn child could not be put to death, that customary plea of pregnant women saved Anne and Mary from the gallows. The governor hanged the other pirates in November 1720, including Anne's lover, handsome Calico Jack.

Mary Read died in jail of typhoid fever. Anne received another reprieve after her daughter's birth, and the rest of her story is unclear.

Some say that former pirate and wealthy planter from Charleston bribed officials to let him take Anne and her child home with him. There they married, and lived quietly the Charleston social life Anne had spurned earlier. Others believe Anne moved west with another man. They settled in the Ohio Valley and lived an exciting life along the wild frontier.

3

STEDE BONNET
THE GENTLEMAN PIRATE

Some of his victims called him "the gentleman pirate." If they lived to tell their tale. His courtly manners and air of breeding set him apart from most pirates.

Stede Bonnet came from a highly respected family in England. He was well-educated, and served as a major in the British army. When he retired in middle age, he and his wife moved to Bridgetown, on the West Indies island of Barbados. They had a busy social life, and considerable wealth from their sugar plantation. Writings from the 1700s describe Bonnet as "a round little man in bright waistcoat and trim breeches, clean-shaven and periwigged."

No one realized that Bonnet had secretly outfitted a ship and gathered a crew of "thugs and rogues" until he suddenly disappeared in early 1717.

His scandalized neighbors spread the word that Bonnet had "gone a pyrating." They muttered and shook their heads. Some said he must have suffered from "a disorder of the mind." Other whispers said that the sharp tongue and whining of his nagging wife caused him to leave in desperation. Perhaps it was the lure of the open sea, or the freedom of life beyond the limits of law and order. Or could it have been that image others had of Bonnet—could he have set out to prove himself a "real man?" Whatever the cause, Bonnet left his rich plantation life to sail under the black flag, the Jolly Roger of piracy. He left Barbados without a word of warning or farewell to anyone.

Since he had never been a seaman, Bonnet had to rely on his seventy derelict hirelings to man his ship, the three-masted sloop, the *Revenge*. With ten cannon lashed to the gun deck, he prowled the Carolina coast from Charleston to Wilmington. In a few days he captured three ships from England and one from Barbados. He plundered the cargos and put the crews ashore. Later he would become more bloodthirsty.

Bonnet's success along the Carolina coast wasn't unusual. Like other pirates, he found there plentiful shipping, and safe inlets and coves for rest and repairs. Bonnet's men met no opposition at Murrells Inlet or Little River and forced the frightened settlers to give them needed supplies.

Blackbeard, the infamous Captain Edward Teach, persuaded Bonnet to join up with him and leave his ship with Blackbeard's crew. After a wild voyage together, Bonnet returned to find the *Revenge* stripped and abandoned. Blackbeard also double-crossed him about the spoils of their voyage. Bonnet had thought of applying for a pardon, but in anger he refitted his ship, renamed it the *Royal James*, and started calling himself Captain Thomas.

Something about the experience with Blackbeard brought out the cruelty in Stede Bonnet. Prisoners were no longer released unharmed. Bonnet allowed his crew to "have fun" torturing captives. According to Hugh F. Rankin in his book, *Pirates of Colonial North Carolina*, Bonnet may have been the only pirate captain to force helpless prisoners to "walk the plank" to their deaths.

Bonnet captured at least ten more prizes along the Carolina coast before the *Royal James* began leaking badly. He sailed north, close to shore, until he reached the Cape Fear River. Creeks and wooded areas there offered safe hiding places to repair the ship, and Southport, located at the mouth of the river, had become a haven for pirates.

Dropping anchor around a curve in a creek, Bonnet and his crew careened the ship. They found extensive rot and damage to the hull. Bonnet decided to overhaul and refurbish the ship, work which could take a couple of months, before setting sail again. The pirates captured a local shallop, broke it up for lumber, and freed the owners. Unfortunately for Bonnet, those men spread the news that a pirate ship was holed up in the creek.

Pirates had disrupted the trade of the port of Charleston practically from its settlement in 1670. When Royal Governor Robert Johnson heard the news about Bonnet's ship, he quickly sent gunboats to make an example of at least one of the pesky pirates. Colonel William Rhett volunteered to command the small fleet.

Rhett and his men were unfamiliar with the shoals and sand

Sketch by John D. Ellington
*Courtesy of the N.C. Division
of Archives and History*

bars in the mouth of the Cape Fear River. The low tide grounded
and stranded them, but not before they had sighted the *Royal James*
farther inland. Rhett used the time to get ready for battle.

At dawn fierce fighting began. It continued through another
low tide and then a high tide. Seven pirates lay dead, and another
five wounded, while twice as many South Carolinians were casualties. Though Bonnet cursed and threatened, the surviving pirates forced him to surrender. Only later did Colonel Rhett
discover that the Captain Thomas he had captured was actually
Stede Bonnet.

The creek where the pirates were captured lies within the city
limits of Southport, North Carolina, and is still known as "Bonnet's Creek."

Rhett took Bonnet and his crew back to Charleston, where
they were tried and sentenced to death. Most of the crew went to

the gallows in November 1718. Bonnet managed to escape. He hid out on Sullivan's Island, at the mouth of Charleston harbor. Colonel Rhett went after him and captured him once more.

Bonnet tried in every way to escape execution. At the end he became a whimpering, sniveling shadow of a man. On December 10, 1718, on White Point Island in Charleston harbor, while holding a little bunch of flowers in his hands, Stede Bonnet, English gentleman, brave soldier, and bold pirate, groveled and wept until the rope snapped his neck. His body, along with those of many other pirates, was buried below the low tide mark at the edge of the marsh.

Piracy is as old as history itself, and traditionally punished by hanging. So ended Bonnet's brief fling at "pyrating."

The Kaminski House Museum, built in 1769
along the Sampit River in Georgetown
Courtesy of Barry McGee

4

GEORGETOWN
HISTORIC SEAPORT

Ask a Georgetown resident where they live and they'll reply, "You'll find us just a few hundred years down the road, on the King's Highway, south of Myrtle Beach." The town's legends and traditions are kept alive by numerous storytellers, ghost hunts, and tours of the enchanting old houses. Georgetown is considered "The Ghost Capital of the South." Around one hundred spooks, specters, and haunts inhabit the buildings of the area.

To maintain its proud past, in Georgetown's Historic District, old buildings are lovingly restored with careful attention to authentic details. At least fifty buildings date from the early 1700s to the 1850s, with official date markers visible to visitors.

Georgetown's history began in 1526, when the first attempted European settlement north of Mexico was founded along Winyah Bay. The Spaniards only stayed six months due to poor leadership, bad luck, fevers, and the lack of help from the Native Americans whom the settlers had mistreated. As the Spaniards sailed away to Hispaniola, the tribes remained: the Sampit, Winyah, Pee Dee, Choppee, Santee, Waccamaw, and others.

The English settled Charleston in 1670, and trade brought a few Indian agents and traders into the Winyah Bay area. The richness of the soil and warm humid climate caused some traders to turn to farming or producing naval stores from pine tree resin. A network of wide, flowing rivers gave access to the Atlantic Ocean, and opened the possibility of developing a rich trading system.

The English founded Georgetown in 1729, the third settlement in the colony (after Charleston and Beaufort). Elisha Screven laid out the town using an open design of square blocks. That's why the Historic District doesn't contain the crooked alleys and lanes found in many old towns. The King's Highway linked Georgetown with the two towns to the south, and with Wilmington to the north, on the Cape Fear River in North Carolina. As more settlers arrived, the deep Winyah Bay became an official port of entry. England assigned a customs officer in 1732. Land grants were available, and the clearing of plantations began.

The lowlands along the rivers proved ideal for planting indigo and rice, crops that made millionaires of planters. They shipped "Carolina Gold" rice worldwide due to growing demand. Indigo was an English bounty crop that was phased out after the American Revolution. An ever increasing number of African slaves carried the burden of labor. Slaves represented eighty-five percent of Georgetown County's population by 1800.

Georgetown's prosperity brought French, Scot, and English

cultures to mingle with the Native Americans and Africans, bringing about a diversity of civilization. Many buildings and houses are of note.

British soldiers occupied the 1765-built Childermas Croft House during the American Revolution and used it as a hospital. Later, in an attempt to get rid of infectious germs, the owners stabled cows in their house. It was a custom of the times.

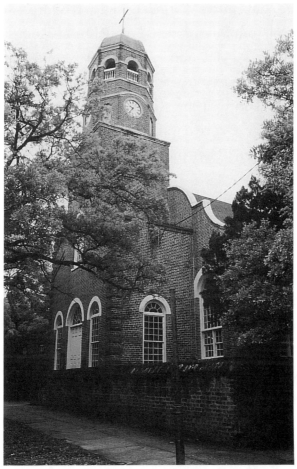

Prince George Winyah Episcopal Church
Courtesy of Barry McGee

Prince George Winyah Episcopal Church, built in 1747, was desecrated in both the Revolution and the Civil War, with horses stabled in the sanctuary. Georgetown has an interesting history from the American Revolution. In November 1780, General Francis Marion, the "Swamp Fox," learned that only fifty British troops garrisoned the town. Marion decided to take it back from the British.

Before he could move, Tories arrived to reinforce the garrison. On November 15th Marion sent Colonel Peter Horry's mounted militia to White's Plantation, where they skirmished with the Tories. Another part of Marion's force under Captain John Melton fought Tories in the swamps near The Pens plantation. Marion's nephew Gabriel was unhorsed and shot dead while trying to surrender. The Americans withdrew after two days of skirmishing.

The Swamp Fox joined with "Lighthorse Harry" Lee's Legion in January 1781 in another attempt to liberate Georgetown. In a carefully planned assault, the infantry of Lee's Legion moved down the Peedee River and hid on an island during the night of January 22-23. The next night they slipped into Georgetown. On the 24th, Lee's cavalry and Marion's partisans charged to link with the infantry. They seized Colonel Campbell, the British commander, but the soldiers in the garrison refused to come to his aid. Instead they stayed in their well-fortified position. With no equipment to attack the garrison, and realizing they would take heavy casualties, the disappointed Marion and Lee paroled Campbell and withdrew.

Francis "Swamp Fox" Marion
Courtesy of the N.C. Division of Archives and History

In late July 1781, partisans under General Thomas Sumter, the "Carolina Gamecock," sought wealth and plundered Loyalist homes. The British responded by virtually destroying George-town. South Carolina Governor John Rutledge ordered the end of "Sumter's Law," which had allowed his men to act with impunity in defiance of the British. This ended Sumter's career.

Plantation owner Robert Stewart built a Georgian brick town-house for his family in 1750. President George Washington stayed there when he visited Georgetown in 1791. The Kaminski House Museum, built in 1769 by Paul Trapier II, stands beside the Stewart House on Front Street. Both face the scenic Sampit River. President Washington also visited the Masonic Lodge, built in the 1700s. Duncan Memorial Methodist Church was organized in the 1780s after a visit by Bishop Francis Asbury.

Planters formed the Winyah Indigo Society in the 1740s as a meeting place and a charity school for the poor. The present building dates from 1857. It is used by the still active society, and for community and private functions.

Georgetown's best known landmark, the Rice Museum, dates to 1842, with the tower added in 1845. Standing tall on Front Street, on the waterfront, this picturesque building tells the story of rice cultivation, of vast fields flooded and drained, and the armies of laborers needed to produce the planters' wealth.

Little is said about the original building, a drab wooden structure where slaves were bought and sold like cattle, beginning in 1788. It's easy to imagine mothers sold away from their children. Fathers, strong field hands, went to other plantations,

Henry "Lighthorse Harry" Lee
Courtesy of the N.C. Division of Archives and History

with little hope of rejoining the families they left. If you listened, could you still hear an echo of the lost cries?

Many ghosts of the Low Country have proven helpful, like the one in the Henning House on Screven Street. A young British officer quartered in an upstairs room of the Henning House during the American Revolution. Loud noises from downstairs awakened him from a nap. He listened and learned the excitement centered around a rumor that Francis Marion had been spotted in Georgetown.

Anxious to help capture the elusive Marion, the young officer dashed from his room to the stairs. He forgot the uneven riser near the top of the steps, and tripped. As he tumbled down the stairs, his head hit hard, snapping his neck.

The officer's fellow soldiers swarmed around their dead comrade, and forgot about the Swamp Fox. Later the British withdrew from Georgetown, but some say the officer's spirit stayed behind.

Now his ghost hovers over the risky stairs, and helps anyone who stumbles.

Almost all the old houses have stories to tell. Visitors often ask about unexplained sounds, like a chair moving, a child crying, or a woman sobbing.

In autumn, people flock to Georgetown for the ghost hunts and tours. With the harvest moon casting eerie shadows, and the night wind sighing through the tree limbs that hang over the cemeteries, and the fog floating in off the bay, and the lights flickering, it is definitely the proper setting for a ghost hunt.

To walk the streets of Georgetown is to breathe history and heritage. Robert Mills, the architect of the Washington Monument, designed the Georgetown Courthouse, which has been used since 1824. From that Greek Revival edifice to a former stand-alone kitchen, moved and restored as a shop, visitors are surrounded by an unhurried atmosphere of ante-bellum days.

5

THE INDEPENDENT REPUBLIC OF HORRY

As more settlers came along the King's Highway and rivers to Georgetown, the village on Winyah Bay grew. Many newcomers claimed land and began to clear plantations farther inland.

In 1734 a small group of daring young men from Georgetown poled their way up the Waccamaw River to Bear Bluff. Since the swampy bays grew ever denser, with no landing place, they turned back. Floating downriver, they noticed a bluff where the river formed a lake. They went ashore. That night they cooked and ate a meal of bear steaks, and made camp on the spot later known as Kingston Bluff. In 1734 it was very lonely country, surrounded by dense swamps full of wild animals.

Today it is the site of Conway, Horry County seat.

In 1985 Horry County celebrated two and a half centuries of settlement. Kingston-on-the-Waccamaw (Conway) was one of eleven townships set up in the Carolina colony in 1730. The aim was to encourage settlers to move inland along the rivers.

Some of the colonists who arrived had traveled down obscure Indian paths from Pennsylvania and Virginia. Others risked their lives by coming on raging rivers. Many were Scots-Irish, lured by the promise of land. They found little to encourage them to stay, but they were schooled in hardships, and stay they did. They worked small farms. The number of settlers was small, but they were close-knit and helped each other. They loaned each other courage.

Their first homes were crude log cabins with mud chimneys and dirt floors, lacking the barest comforts. No house or building still stands from those days in the 1700s, because as soon as possible, the settlers tore down the primitive structures and built improved ones. Hard labor cleared fields to produce food.

With no money crop, the main industry was the production of turpentine from the dense forests of yellow pine trees. J. W. Ogilvie, writing for *The Horry Herald* in 1900, characterized the turpentine industry as "scraping a pine tree." The lumber industry developed later. According to Ogilvie, living conditions for succeeding generations were the most primitive imaginable. There was poverty, hardships, and disasters, but the people coped and adapted.

The entire family helped produce corn, peas, collards, turnips, beans, and potatoes. Stalks of sugar cane yielded syrup for "sweetenin'."

The settlers brought their own customs, religious beliefs, and skills. They struggled to make meals nutritious and enjoyable, a difficult task since so few foods were available. Many recipes were Old Country favorites: gingerbread from the Lake District of England, treacle scones from Scotland, tattie soup from Ireland, oxtail stew from Germany, and apple pandowdy from England.

Other dishes had New World titles: Indian pudding, Boston baked beans, and pumpkin pie.

The best river land had been granted to people who did not settle in the township and use the land. Much of the other soil was poor and unsuited to farming. Somehow the little village on the Waccamaw survived. The settlers asked for and received little help. They were self-sufficient, with a spirit of sturdy independence. Why should they mind the British or pay taxes to a faraway government in London? This spirit reigned in Horry County long before the signing of the Declaration of Independence in 1776.

A unique life style and attitude developed because of the region's location and isolation. The people were full of pride and slow to change. A title from the 1880s described the area as "The Independent Republic of Horry." Whether true or not, the title reflects the strength and self-sufficiency of a proud populace who carved a home out of the wilderness. They always held onto visions of better times to come.

The coastal region was swampy, with fast-flowing creeks, rivers, and fresh water lakes. The areas called "bays" were low and boggy, unfit for cultivation or building sites. Hunters found among the wild animals black bears, deer, and flocks of birds. Rivers and creeks teemed with fish. The bays supported jungle-like growth in the mire. People were lost in the bays and never found, including one fleeing pirate in the early 1700s.

In 1801 the region became Horry County, to honor General Peter Horry, aide to General Francis Marion, and a hero during

Peter Horry
Used by permission of the Horry County Museum

the American Revolution.

Layers of shale and quicksand made road building almost impossible, so there were few coastal trails. Access was mainly by river to Murrells Inlet or Little River. Because of the lack of access, the beaches weren't settled until the early 1900s.

Geographical conditions along the King's Highway range from the white sands of the beaches to the bays, swamps, and half-drowned tidal river lands. Higher and drier land lies north and west of Conway. Horry County has always been dominated by its rivers, and it was further divided by the construction of the Intracoastal Waterway in 1936. The Lumber and Pee Dee rivers form the western and southern boundaries, effectively cutting the county off from the rest of the state. The first narrow wooden bridge across the Pee Dee at Galivants Ferry was built in 1902, for travel into Marion County.

Horry County has come a long way from being the most isolated and under-developed part of South Carolina. It has become a center of tourism for the nation. Those hardy Scotch-Irish settlers who ventured down the rivers and the King's Highway over two hundred and fifty years ago wouldn't have believed it.

6

PLANTATIONS

All I want in this creation
Is a pretty little wife—
And a big plantation.

Anonymous

Many settlers came to the southern colonies, dreaming of owning a plantation and living the life of a rich planter. In the early days, the rice planters became the incredibly wealthy ones. According to Professor Lewis P. Jones in his book *South Carolina, One of the Fifty States*, there were 559 rice planters in the United States by 1850; 446 were in South Carolina.

Thousands of slaves strained to clear the land and grow the rice for a demanding European market. The coastal tidewater region was ideal for flooding rice fields; ocean tides pushed fresh water inland for ten to thirty-five miles, providing an unfailing supply.

Rice cultivation centered on rivers and creeks around Georgetown. Waccamaw Neck, extending from the Waccamaw River to the Atlantic Ocean, had thirteen plantations cleared and planted by 1760. At the height of the rice production, before the Civil War, Georgetown County had 162 plantations.

The naming of houses, farms, and estates in England was a centuries old custom. Colonists saw no reason to change the custom in the New World. Some names, like Hobcaw Barony, Hopsewee, and Wachesaw, came from Indian tribes in the region.

Brookgreen was named for a stream surrounded by green meadows, near Hammersmith in Middlesex, England. Waverly Plantation got its name from Sir Walter Scott's "Waverly" novels. Rossdhu bears the name of an owner's ancestral Scottish home. Windsor Plantation, located on the Black River, took the name of Windsor Castle on the Thames River, the home of English sovereigns since William the Conqueror. In Old English, Windsor means "winding shore."

Beneventum Plantation's name came from the Latin phrase meaning, "good come to you." Others were named for towns or regions: Hagley for the town in Worcester, England; Arcadia for the peaceful countryside in Greece; Calais for the town in France; and Dover for the site on the English Channel.

Arundel Plantation bears the name of a castle on the Arun River in Sussex, England. Dirleton bears the name of a castle in Scotland. Rose Bank Plantation came from Rosebank, on the Tweed River in Kelso, Scotland.

Cat Island, reached only by boat, lies between Winyah Bay and the North Santee River. The island, which held four plantations, got its name from the large number of wild cats. The Cat Island Rig, one of the few ferries left, moves across the water, as one passenger expressed it, "by the grace of Gawd." The ferry has been known to dump its cargo.

No one knows whether Forlorn Hope Plantation got its name because of the Allston family's military service, or the task of making fields and crops from a dismal river swamp.

White House Plantation, located near the junction of the Black and Pee Dee rivers, got its name from the small white house that

Joel Roberts Poinsett
Courtesy of the N.C. Division of Archives and History

sits in the middle of a cleared field. Its owner, widowed Mary Izzard Pringle, married Joel Roberts Poinsett in the 1840s. They remodeled the house, and Poinsett developed beautiful gardens nearby. To escape the Low Country heat and humidity, they spent the summers at Poinsett's home on Old White Horse Road, near Greenville.

Poinsett, an outstanding statesman, had served as U. S. Minister to Mexico. He unsuccessfully tried to buy Texas from Mexico under presidents John Quincy Adams and Andrew Jackson. Among the plants he brought back to South Carolina was a wild weed that he found interesting. From it he developed a flower that bloomed at Christmas. The Poinsettia bears his name.

The name of Hasty Point Plantation, on the Pee Dee River, dates to an American Revolution tradition. The "Swamp Fox," General Francis Marion, was a constant thorn in the Redcoats' side, striking out of nowhere, raiding and confusing his enemies, then disappearing into the swamps. In 1780, after the fall of Charleston and the disastrous American defeat at Camden, Marion and his men kept the revolution alive in South Carolina while Nathaniel Greene reorganized the American army. Marion established his main camp at Snow's Island, a low ridge along the Pee Dee. The British launched a serious campaign to wipe out the partisans.

One day Marion, with, as usual, the British in hot pursuit, raced down the bank of the Pee Dee and jumped into a canoe. The Swamp Fox paddled off into the river, then turned up a small creek.

The British finally found a boat and tried to follow Marion, but he had disappeared. The Redcoats mistakenly entered Thoroughfare Creek, which swiftly carried their boat into the Waccamaw River toward Georgetown. Once more, they had failed to catch the Swamp Fox. The constant setbacks made one British commander complain that Marion "would not fight like a gentleman or a Christian."

The plantation near the point where Marion made his hasty canoe escape became Hasty Point.

7

INDIGO BLUE

The word "indigo" comes from the name India, the country where the plant originated. Traders brought the seeds to Europe as early as the days of the Roman Empire. The Romans used indigo dye and the seeds spread through Europe and England in the first century A.D. The dye was so rich and vibrant, it was fit for royalty. Even today the shade is called "royal blue."

Textile mills in England and Europe caused a demand for indigo dye in the 1700s. The plant grew best in semi-tropical lands. The Caribbean Islands produced the dye, but France and Spain, who owned the islands, were often at war and not trading. England urged the southern American colonies to grow indigo as a bounty crop. Few planters tried it.

Sixteen-year-old Eliza Lucas moved with her family in 1738 to a plantation near Charleston. Her father, the governor of Antigua, also owned land on the Waccamaw and Black Rivers. After building a fine home of "tabby" (an oyster shell and lime material), Governor Lucas was called back to Antigua. He left Eliza in charge of his plantations. With the help of the overseers, she managed well, and the workers and slaves loved her. They called her "Young Missy."

Eliza learned of the bounty offer for indigo, and began experimenting with seeds her father sent. It took three years of failure before she grew a good crop. She sent a fine grade of dye to her agent in England, and shared her knowledge and seeds with other planters.

Producing dye from the weed-like plants was complicated. The leaves, covered with water in a huge vat, quickly decayed in the hot climate, creating an odor so bad that people said you could smell an indigo plantation an hour before you saw it. Eliza and the planters said they didn't mind; it was the smell of money.

The water, drained from the rotted leaves into clean vats, went through heating and cooling cycles and into evaporation pans. There the solution dried into gray-white sheets, which were cut into wafers and packed for shipment. The depth of blue color on cloth depended on the amount of water and wafer used.

Once the process was well-known, backwoods farmers often grew a few plants for home use. The dye brightened up the "linsey-woolsey" or cotton fabrics they spun and wove into cloth. Francis Withers reportedly grew indigo near Withers Lake, which lies beyond the saltwater Withers Swash, along the Grand Strand.

Vast fortunes were made in Georgetown County from growing indigo before the American Revolution.

In the late 1740s a group of planters began to meet in Georgetown. They received a Royal Charter in 1758 as the Winyah Indigo Society. The club enjoyed eating, drinking, and discussing their problems and successes. They used their dues to set up schools in Georgetown and the back country for poor children.

The bounty payment and market for indigo in England stopped after the Revolution. With the crop less profitable, planters shifted to growing rice and cotton.

The South Carolina state flag, adopted in 1775, used the royal blue color. Perennial indigo plants still grow wild near old fields, but the crop is no longer important.

A popular song of earlier days used the name "Mood Indigo" to express the depression of lost love. Names along the Grand Strand include Indigo Farms, Indigo Lakes, Indigo Wells Golf Course, Indigo Inn, and Indigo Creek Real Estate Company. One owner named his land holdings "True Blue Plantation."

Lovely and determined Eliza Lucas married Charles Pinckney in 1744. She called him "Mr. Pinckney" since he was almost twice her age, but she loved him dearly. They had two sons, Thomas and Charles Cotesworth Pinckney, both of whom went to England for education as lawyers. Both later became prominent in state and the new national government. Eliza and Charles had a daughter, Harriott, who married Daniel Horry of Hampton Plantation on the Santee River.

Charles Pinckney died in 1758. During the American Revolution, Eliza's plantations near Charleston were destroyed and her home burned. She moved in with her daughter at Hampton Plantation and lived there until her death.

Thomas Lynch, Jr.
Courtesy of the N.C. Division of Archives and History

8

HOPSEWEE PLANTATION

To visit Hopsewee Plantation is to take a step back in time, to the historic past of South Carolina's Coastal Plain. King George II of England granted the land to the Lynch family in 1677. Four families have owned the property and lived there. They cherished it as their home, and lovingly preserved it through the centuries. The property has never suffered from neglect or decay.

Mr. and Mrs. James T. Maynard currently own Hopsewee and live in it year-round. They care for the property, preserve its charm and heritage, and make it available for all to visit and enjoy.

The manor house sits dreaming atop a high bank of the North Santee River, which flows past on its journey from the North Carolina mountains to the Atlantic Ocean. The house is a classic example of plantation architecture, as a "four-square" design. It had four rooms downstairs, with a wide hall separating them, a stairway, and four rooms upstairs. Each room contains hand-carved molding. Scored tabby, crushed oyster shells and lime, cover the brick foundation. The black cypress walls of the house will last for centuries.

The name "Hopsewee" comes from the days of Indian migrations to the coast. "Hop" was the name of a Cherokee tribal chief. The Sewee tribe lived south of Georgetown. The Lynches combined the two names.

Thomas Lynch, Sr. built the manor house in the 1730s. His son, Thomas, Jr. was born there. The boy slept at night in the top of the big house, enjoying his view of the river through windows of hand-blown glass. Thomas, Jr. knew that someday he would manage a rice plantation. He played in the woods and along the river banks, and learned to hunt and fish with slave companions.

In 1762 the family moved across the river, opposite Hopsewee, to Peachtree Plantation. Soon after, at age fifteen, Thomas, Jr. sailed for England. For ten years he pursued a "proper education" for a young man of his class. He attended Eton College, and studied law at Middle Temple. However, when he returned home, instead of practicing law, he settled into the comfortable life of a planter.

Lynch and his father were both elected delegates to the Second Continental Congress in 1776. They traveled to Philadelphia to discuss the monumental decision on whether the colonies should declare independence from Great Britain. Thomas Lynch, Jr. voted to accept the Declaration of Independence, and signed the document along with three other South Carolinians: Edward Rutledge, Thomas Heyward, Jr., and Arthur Middleton. A fifth space remained for Thomas Lynch, Sr., but he suffered a stroke and was unable to sign.

The British captured Charleston in 1780. Among their captives were the other three signers of the Declaration. The British sent the three to prison in St. Augustine. Thomas Lynch, Jr. was in North Carolina at the time, recruiting soldiers. He had avoided capture, but he came down with the dreaded swamp fever.

Lynch and his wife wanted to get him away from the swamps so he could recover. They secretly boarded a ship bound for France. The vessel sailed out into the Atlantic, and was never heard from again.

Hopsewee Manor House sits atop a bank on the North Santee River
Courtesy of Barry McGee

No one knows the fate of one of our nation's Founding Fathers. Hopsewee Plantation, Lynch's birthplace, still sits above the river, as it has for over two and a half centuries. Its dignity and beauty remained unchanged, a National Historic Landmark for all to see.

9

PEACHTREE MANOR

The ruins of Peachtree Manor House can still be seen from Hopsewee Plantation, across the North Santee River. Though the house burned in 1840, the high brick walls, gaping windows, massive steps and ironwork, along with remnants of yellow pine timbers all demonstrate the expert craftsmanship that went into the house's building.

In 1762 Thomas Lynch, Sr. decided to move his family from the birthplace of his son, Thomas Lynch, Jr., to a more favorable location. So the Lynches left Hopsewee and moved across the river to Peachtree Manor. It was from this house that the thirty-year-old son and his wife left for a sea voyage, and never returned.

Some years before the house burned, another owner of Peachtree lived there with his wife and lovely eighteen-year-old daughter. One day a Spanish ship sailed up the South Santee River with the high tide, and stopped at the Peachtree landing. The captain asked permission to leave a sick seaman there, while the ship went on to Charleston. The sailor had the dreaded yellow fever.

The planter answered no.

He feared the yellow fever, and knew it would bring tragedy

to his family. However his daughter insisted that they must act humanely and take care of the sick man. She had him taken to the Sick House, a building they used to treat ill slaves. The daughter nursed the sailor herself. Though she fought to keep him alive, the sailor only lived three days. The ship never returned, so they buried the man on their land.

Predictably, the lovely daughter fell ill with the yellow fever.

When she died, the mother was inconsolable. The father lost his mind.

No friends or neighbors were allowed in Peachtree House. Alone, the father built a coffin and prepared his lost daughter for burial. He carried the coffin deep into a thicket of fragrant wild bushes, which his daughter had always loved. The father set the coffin upright on the ground, and began to dig.

Except the thought of his precious child underground was more than he could stand. Instead of digging a hole, he started piling dirt up the sides of the coffin.

The plantation slaves, who had also loved the daughter, watched with deep sorrow the father work. One by one, they silently slipped up to form a circle, and helped to pile the dirt.

When they covered the top of the coffin, they didn't stop. The mound rose to a height of fifteen feet, an earthen pyramid in the wilds of the Carolina Coast.

And the mound has stood for a century and a half. It is no longer as tall, having gradually sunk into the ground. Bushes and pines grow from it. Yet the sacred spot remains a symbol of a father's devotion and grief.

10

HAMPTON PLANTATION

Through the tall windows on three sides of the elegant ball-room at Hampton Plantation, one could look toward the lovely gardens and the Santee River. If guests arrived by boat for the evening, flickering torches lighted the walkways from the river. Carriage wheels announced the arrival of guests who had traveled along the King's Highway from neighboring plantations. In ante-bellum days, a festive social life marked the season when the plantation families were in residence.

The central part of Hampton House, a four-square farmhouse, was built in the 1730s. The Horry family claimed the land as early as 1686. They were among the French Huguenots who settled along the Santee River when they fled persecution in France. Daniel Horry and his wife, Judith Serre, built the house. They lived there until Judith and their two children died. In 1768 Daniel married Harriott Pinckney, daughter of Charles and Eliza Lucas Pinckney. Daniel died in 1785. With both husbands gone, Harriott and Eliza lived together at Hampton.

In the late 1780s they added the ballroom, a two-storied master bedroom, and a wide front portico, with eight massive pillars supporting the roof. The floor of the forty-two-foot ballroom was

This is a 1790 portrait of President George Washington
Courtesy of the N.C. Division of Archives and History

wide, heart pine boards, all cut to the same length. Cypress paneling lined the walls. The seven-foot fireplace was faced with Delft tiles, in color, depicting various beautiful scenes. It had a marble hearth. The arched ceiling stood twenty-eight feet high.

In 1791 news came of an important event: the Southern Tour of President George Washington. Eliza and her family were old friends of the president, so, of course he had to visit Hampton on his journey. Invitations went out. Eliza and Harriott made plans for a gala celebration.

Friends from nearby plantations, Georgetown, and Charleston all made arrangements to attend. Eliza's two sons had both served as officers in the Continental Army under Washington, and planned to come. One of them, Charles Cotesworth Pinckney, had signed the Constitution.

Washington's party spent the night in Georgetown, then started down the King's Highway. The journey was difficult since they had to cross rivers and creeks, but they arrived before noon. A great crowd watched as Washington's "chariot" creaked down the long drive toward Hampton House, followed by his entire entourage. They all straightened their coats or dresses, and checked their hair. A favored group of ladies waited on the great porch as the president was ushered from his coach and up the front steps. The ladies all wore stylish dresses, with sashes and head bandeaux inscribed with the words: "Hail to the Father of Our Country."

As the ladies chatted with the president, someone called his attention to an oak tree several feet from the front steps. When asked if it should be cut, Washington replied, "Let it stand!" Over two hundred years later, the tree still stands. Called the "Washington Oak," it shades a 115-foot circle of the yard.

The bountiful brunch for the president and guests was served in the great ballroom. Long tables, bright with snowy linen, china, silver, and flowers, stood loaded with every imaginable delicacy. Washington's visit was a success for everyone involved.

When Eliza fell ill in 1793, her children insisted on taking her to doctors in Philadelphia. President Washington was among the first to call on her. Eliza died on May 27, 1793. One of her pallbearers, at his own request, was the president.

Through the years the property passed to descendants of the

Charles Cotesworth Pinckney, signer of the Constitution
Courtesy of the N.C. Division of Archives and History

original family. Archibald Rutledge inherited Hampton Planta-tion in 1923. He left his teaching position in Pennsylvania in 1937 to restore the old house and grounds, a monumental task. The house had been unoccupied for nearly two decades, although friends had looked after it, planted the fields, and managed to keep

The mansion at Hampton Plantation; to the right is the "Washington Oak"
Courtesy of Barry McGee

the place from succumbing to the near-tropical growth of the Santee swamps. Rutledge's book *Home by the River* gives a fascinating account of his work and life at Hampton. His love for the 2000-acre plantation shows through in every paragraph.

Because of his national literary reputation, the South Carolina legislature named Rutledge Poet Laureate in 1934. He kept that title until his death in 1973. Hampton was the inspiration for nearly all of his writing. In 1971 he sold the house and 310 acres to the state to insure its preservation and continued protection.

When he returned in 1937 to live at Hampton, Rutledge repaired a Chippendale armchair that stood by the fireplace in the parlor. As a boy, Rutledge had asked his father about the broken chair. His father explained:

In the late 1770s, during the American Revolution, a frequent guest at Hampton Plantation was General Francis Marion. He visited for rest and refreshment. One day, exhausted, Marion sat nodding in the armchair by the fire. A troop of British soldiers rode up into the yard. Instantly alert, Marion saw through the window that the soldiers were led by Colonel Banastre Tarleton. "Bloody" Tarleton, Marion's arch-enemy, would certainly have no mercy on the Swamp Fox. British General Cornwallis so worried about Marion's partisans that he ordered Tarleton's Legion to find and destroy them.

That day at Hampton, Marion jumped up and knocked over the chair. The left arm broke away from the back.

A low door stood near the fireplace, and fortunately Marion was small enough to fit through. Then a secret door led to a passageway and the back of the house. Marion made it outside, leapt onto his horse, and galloped away. He swam the river to the delta and made his way back to Georgetown County.

The wily Swamp Fox had once again turned the tables on Bloody Tarleton. Tarleton was reported to have later said, after finally giving up on catching Marion, "As for this damned old fox, the devil himself could not catch him!"

Owners of Hampton Plantation kept the Chippendale armchair as it was, broken, for nearly 160 years in honor of the event.

Like most of the plantations, Hampton has its own ghost tale. It's such a great story, it had to be a separate chapter.

Hampton Plantation was the thirty-eighth state park in South Carolina. Lying across the Santee River, south of Georgetown, the park is open to visitors. Hampton House is listed on the National Register of Historic Places.

11

THE GHOST OF JOHN HENRY
AT HAMPTON PLANTATION

It was the spring of 1830. John Henry Rutledge, twenty-one years old and heir to Hampton Plantation, was in love.

John Henry reined in his horse along Georgetown's Front Street at the apothecary shop. He had ridden hard along the King's Highway from Hampton, a distance of about sixteen miles. As he got off his horse, he scarcely noticed the people on the street speaking to him. He had problems. Now he hoped to talk to his love's father, and find an ally.

Young John Henry knew the rules of life. The most important one was that no young person ever married beneath them; such a spouse could never take a proper place in society. John Henry had no problem with that rule—until he fell in love with a pharmacist's daughter.

She was young and pretty. After he discovered her, he rode into Georgetown at every opportunity to see and talk to her. Not only was she a "winsome lass," but she was educated and well-mannered. John Henry thought her far superior to the girls on the plantations that he'd known all his life.

Surely there could be an exception to the marrying-beneath-you rule.

He had gone to his mother, Harriott Horry Rutledge, and told her about his love for the girl in a long and earnest speech. He bared his heart. Surely she would understand.

His mother had married late, when she was nearly thirty. Her own mother, Harriott Pinckney Horry, had feared that her only daughter would end up a spinster. Instead she eloped with Frederick Rutledge. Now she had a large family, four boys and four girls, to train and groom for their life as planters. Her word was law, and the children acted accordingly.

Harriott was horrified at the thought of John Henry marrying a pharmacist's daughter. She bluntly told him that his duty to the family meant he had to have a "good" marriage.

John Henry's brothers and sisters were no help to him. The Rutledges were no different from any other family—siblings were jealous, especially of the heir-apparent to the rich Hampton Plantation. The brothers and sisters teased and taunted John Henry: "Why don't you grow up? You're young! You should have lots of girls before you marry. Find another one—there are lots around. Who do you think you are, trying to change the rules?"

With everyone against him, John Henry went into his room alone. He pulled a rocker over to the window where he could gaze at the fields of home he had always loved. Yet he could find no joy in them now. He felt only sorrow, and tears wet his cheeks.

He brooded over his problem, and grew angry. He decided his family couldn't stop his happiness. When they got to know his "Lady Love," they would love her too.

So he decided to talk to the girl's father. He would tell of his devotion, of his family's objections, and how he planned to marry the girl anyway and take her to live at Hampton. That's what had brought John Henry to the apothecary shop in Georgetown that spring day.

He poured out his heart to the pharmacist. To young John Henry, there was no way the father could do anything but understand and cooperate.

The father saw it differently.

He rejected John Henry, his family, estate, and his high and mighty plan. Angrily he said that he would never allow his precious daughter to marry into a family that would look down upon her.

Furthermore, John Henry was no longer welcome in his shop, or even on his side of Front Street.

The tables had turned. John Henry couldn't believe it. A Rutledge spurned? He sadly mounted his horse and rode back to Hampton. Then he went to his room, sat in his rocker, and stared out the window.

The Rutledge family was tired of John Henry's behavior and his depression. He had brought his sorrow on himself, and he must learn his lesson. They ignored him. His mother and father worried about him, but they wore a stony face and refused to look at him. John Henry sat alone in his room and rocked.

On the stormy night of March 30, 1830, John Henry made another decision. He got out his pistol, and sat in his chair. He stared blankly at the wind and rain that beat against his window. The weather was like the world, uncaring.

John Henry slowly raised the gun to his head.

All he had wanted was to love a beautiful young woman. How could anyone deny him that?

His finger put a little pressure on the trigger.

Why hadn't anyone understood?

The gun fired.

John Henry sagged to the floor. Blood splattered over his room, puddling on the floorboards.

His family ran to investigate. And cried out in agony.

He was still alive. Barely. They sent for the doctor.

Now the Rutledge family rallied around John Henry. For two days he hung between life and death. Finally he took his last breath.

The Rutledge family sadly laid their troubled son to rest in a corner of the garden facing the Santee River. They marked his grave with a white marble slab.

But the spirit of John Henry didn't rest.

Over the years, many visitors at Hampton Plantation have entered the room where he sat, and felt his presence. Though it's empty, from time to time the chair rocks. The family sanded away the blood stains on the floor, but they came back. They tried again, and again, and many more times. The stains always returned. Some people have heard a cry of agony, perhaps John

Henry's anguish at an unforgiving world, or his death scream as he squeezed the trigger.

John Henry's spirit is a restless one. Perhaps he still seeks the love he so desired, or maybe he just wants understanding. His siblings might advise him: "Give it up, John Henry. Rest in peace."

12

PAWLEYS ISLAND

Without a doubt, nature and history combined to create a special place, the "arrogantly shabby" beach resort known as Pawleys Island. Its visitors have included roving Indian tribes, early settlers, pirates, Colonial travelers, British invaders, Civil War blockade runners, riverboat traders, and happy vacationers.

Ranking as one of the smallest of the coastal islands, Pawleys is about four miles long and one-fourth mile wide. Thousands of years of tides, winds, and storms carved and shaped this piece of land, raising it a bit above sea level. Its sandy beach fronts on the great Atlantic Ocean. Behind it lies a marshy run of water that delights boaters and fishermen. Pawleys is a mecca for those who like to watch birds, turtles, and 'gators, or catch shrimp and crabs.

In 1711 Percival Pawley and his three sons received a land grant from the king of England. Their thousands of acres included coast, marshes, river swamps, bays, thickly wooded areas, and fertile soil. The grant stretched from the Atlantic to the Waccamaw River. The King's Highway ran through it.

Slaves toiled in the heat to clear the land. Then they planted rice, and used the rivers and creeks to flood the fields.

The plantation owners along the King's Highway built fine homes with lavish furnishings for their families. They used small boats on the waterways to visit or send messages. Luxuriant entertaining, visiting, and celebrating took place during the winter months.

Summers were different.

Stagnant water over rice fields and swamps caused disease-bearing mosquitoes to breed in vast swarms. Back then no one knew that mosquitoes spread the dreaded "swamp fever" or "summer fever." The well-off just knew to leave in the hot times. They developed a pattern of an annual migration to the shore or mountains.

Pawleys Island was an ideal summer retreat. It was close. It lay beyond the salt marshes that separated the island from the soggy river lands. Many prominent families found relief on the island from the three or four hot, humid, summer months.

The planters built simple, shelter-type houses on Pawleys. Cyprus trees from the marshes made durable lumber that could withstand the elements. Plantation workers cut the lumber, and transported the building materials by boat. They erected cottages quickly behind the high sand dunes along the wide beach.

The comfortable, casual living meant the families took their furnishings and supplies with them, including house slaves and nurses for the children. Sometimes they would travel the river ferries and bad roads to visit Georgetown or Charleston. The men left when necessary to conduct business. The women and children preferred the beach.

Today, Pawleys Island has somehow escaped the haphazard development seen on other parts of the coast. The island even has a famous resident ghost, the Gray Man, who reportedly warns people of disastrous storms.

Most of the early-1800 structures have fallen prey to storms over the years, but a few sea-weathered cottages remain, still nestled behind the protective dunes. Pawleys Island cast a spell on those early visitors. They always hurried back.

The South Carolina Flag

13

THE SOUTH CAROLINA STATE FLAG

It's a proud flag. With its royal blue background and white crescent and palmetto tree, it's simplicity is classic. The South Carolina state flag always flies in eighth place when the original thirteen colonies' flags are displayed, to signify the state's May 23, 1788 ratification of the Constitution.

As the colonies went to war with England in 1775, patriots pulled down British flags. South Carolina's royal governor took refuge on a British warship in the Charleston harbor. Groups of men met to discuss independence in Kingston and Georgetown districts, and all over the colony.

The South Carolina Revolutionary Council of Safety asked Colonel William Moultrie to design a flag for use by the soldiers manning the forts along the coast. Moultrie chose a rectangle of royal blue, the color of the soldiers' uniforms and the dye of the indigo plant. Taking the symbol on the men's caps, Moultrie fashioned a simple white crescent for the flag's upper corner, near the flagstaff.

In June 1776, horses' hooves and carriages covered the King's Highway as families fled Charleston for the safety of plantation homes. The British fleet had arrived. South Carolina would be an example to the other rebellious colonies.

William Moultrie
*Courtesy of the N.C. Division
of Archives and History*

The British anchored opposite Sullivan's Island, where a fort was about half-completed by the rebels. Lacking stones for the fort's walls, Col. Moultrie had used what he had. The Sabal Palmetto, the official state tree of South Carolina, grows along the coast from North Carolina down to Florida. The tree's name comes from the Spanish word *palmito,* which means small palm. Moultrie constructed parallel walls of palmetto logs, and filled the sixteen-foot space between them with sand. When the British fleet opened fire on Fort Sullivan on June 28, 1776, at 11 a.m., the 2nd South Carolina and the 4th Artillery manned the fort, a total of 435 men. More than one hundred enemy guns blasted away at the Americans, but the spongy palmetto logs didn't shatter like ordinary wood, and the sand cushioned the impact of the cannon balls. Short on powder and ammunition, the rebel gunners slowly returned fire with deadly accuracy. British Commodore Peter Parker's flagship, the *Bristol*, suffered more than seventy hits.

A cannon ball struck the flag designed by Moultrie. It fell outside the fort. Though shells and cannon balls rained all around him, Sergeant William Jasper went out through a gun embrasure, retrieved the flag, improvised a new staff, and planted the flag on the fort's walls. The men cheered.

The British gave up that night and sailed away, having suffered a humiliating defeat. Rebel morale skyrocketed.

For his bravery, Sgt. Jasper received a sword from South Carolina Governor John Rutledge, and was offered a commission. He declined due to his lack of education. Originally from the Georgetown area, Jasper served as a roving scout under Moultrie and Generals Francis Marion and Benjamin Lincoln. He died while planting the colors of the 2nd South Carolina on the Spring Hill redoubt in the assault on Savannah in October 1779. A monument honors him at Savannah, and a redoubt on Sullivan's Island was renamed for him.

The palmetto tree was later added to the state seal on the flag to honor the battle of Sullivan's Island. A full-size bronze and cast iron replica of the tree stands on the capital grounds in Columbia, a memorial to the South Carolina Palmetto Regiment, who fought valiantly in the Mexican War of 1846.

South Carolina's flag design is not an artist's concept. It is an image etched in the blood of battle. The death and suffering of loyal men and women brought it into being. It is a proud symbol of the proud Palmetto State.

William Bartram
Courtesy of the N.C. Division of Archives and History

14

THE BARTRAM TRAIL

As he traveled along the King's Highway in the fall of 1776, William Bartram wrote that he found very few inns or public houses along the coast. However, the few people who had settled there welcomed visitors bringing news of other places. They warmly received Bartram. His hosts were in awe of the sketches he made, and his delight in plants. They had never seen anyone so "daft" about plain old trees.

William Bartram was born in Philadelphia in 1739, the fifth of nine sons of Quaker farmer John Bartram. One day, as John plowed a field, he stopped when he spotted a daisy. The plant's simplicity and beauty inspired him to spend the rest of his life exploring and collecting all forms of nature. King George III of England appointed John Bartram in 1765 Royal Botanist in America. He held this position until his death in 1777. William showed an early interest in natural sciences, and accompanied his father on several of his trips. He displayed great talent at drawing natural objects.

Benjamin Franklin offered young William a position as his apprentice printer, but William chose to train as a merchant and settled for a while at Cape Fear, North Carolina. He also tried farming. Nature called him back to its study.

William accompanied his father in 1765-66 on an exploration in Florida. His drawings caught the attention of the famous English botanist, Dr. John Fothergill. In return for collecting and sending to England seeds and specimens, Fothergill agreed to finance an exploration of the southeastern part of America.

In 1773 William Bartram left on a four-year journey through eight southern colonies. As he traveled north from Charleston to the Grand Strand, Bartram visited the unusual coquina formation that is now Hurl Rocks Park in Myrtle Beach. He described them as "Cliffs of Rocks."

Bartram discovered that the natural vegetation was plentiful and varied. A few palmettos and yuccas were mixed in with the native yaupon, holly, and myrtle. Forests of pines, oaks, gums, and cyprus flourished.

In secluded spots deep in the upper Waccamaw swamps, Bartram identified and wrote about the rare Venus Flytrap. This plant, unique to the area, grows in bogs lacking in nitrogen, and ingests insects to supply this deficiency. The hinged upper part of each blossom allows it to close tightly when an insect wanders in.

Bartram found the northern limits of the magnificent Magnolia Grandiflora in this area. He identified the sweet bay tree, which flourishes in the bays and swamps of the Waccamaw River. He drew and described the plants in vivid detail.

Although Bartram's intent was to record the region's animal

and plant life, he also detailed the people in the early southern colonies, including the Native Americans.

In 1791 Bartram published his *Travels*, an account of his journey through the southeast. Critics hailed the book as both a work of literature and an important scientific achievement. The romantic writers Wordsworth and Coleridge used the book as a source of information. *Travels* went into many foreign editions, and today is considered an American natural history classic.

Thomas Jefferson asked William Bartram in 1803 to accompany Lewis and Clark on their exploration of the Louisiana Territory. Bartram recorded numerous botanical observations on the journey.

Courtesy of J. K. Floyd

Upon the death of John Bartram, his Botanic garden passed to William and brother John. As partners, they established the first nursery in the United States, and printed the first plant catalog. Thomas Jefferson bought their plants for Monticello. The Continental Congress adjourned a 1784 session so the members could tour the garden and nursery.

Other scientists who traveled the King's Highway include Mark Catesby, a British botanist. In 1722 he illustrated a *Natural History of Carolina, Florida, and the Bahamas.* He told of the surprise of finding pink dogwoods in the coastal swamps of South Carolina.

John James Audubon traveled the Highway in the early 1800s. He was delighted by the wildlife he observed in the deep swamps and the lagoon-like bays. In his notes he described yellow jessamine and white dogwood, with sweet bay and magnolia scenting the air. He found the variety of birds and animals too numerous to list.

William Bartram died in 1823. He had explored more of America than any other scientist of his time. Across South Carolina, from the mountains to the sea, five historic markers show the route he traveled in his journeys of discovery.

15

FLORENA BUDWIN

THE CAPTAIN'S ORDERLY

Florence National Cemetery is sometimes called "Little Arlington" because veterans of six wars are buried there. It is located on National Cemetery Road in South Florence, across from the site of the old Confederate prisoner of war camp.

Florena Budwin lies in this shrine. This is her story.

*   *   *

On a cold winter day in 1862, the United States Army directed Joseph Budwin to report for active duty. He had previously served in the army, and his rank of captain would be reinstated. Joseph and his wife, Florena, had expected the notice to come ever since the Southern states' secession and the First Battle of Bull Run. Joseph Budwin had sworn to do his duty, but he didn't want to leave his wife. She had no family to turn to. Their little farm near Philadelphia was isolated, so there were no neighbors to depend on.

That night Joseph sat with Florena by the fire, discussing their problem. Suddenly Joseph had an idea. Florena listened closely, her eyes glued to her husband's face. She nodded agreement. The fire had died to piles of gray ash before they finally went to bed.

In late January 1863, Joseph Budwin reported to his superior officer:

"Captain Joseph Budwin, sir, reporting for duty. Frank Brown, who wishes to enlist, will serve as my orderly, sir." Captain Budwin motioned toward the slim young man who stood silently beside him. The major nodded and handed over some papers for the captain and his orderly to sign. Nervous, holding his breath, Frank Brown signed his name and joined the army. Frank Brown was, of course, Florena Budwin. She saluted the major and followed her captain to his quarters.

As his orderly, Florena served her husband faithfully. She prepared his meals, blacked his boots, cleaned his uniform, and cared for his horses. She slept on a pallet inside his tent. Fortunately the rough foot soldiers serving under Budwin paid little attention to the sissy lad who took care of their captain.

Months passed, and the Budwins proved experts at hiding their true feelings. Joseph unobtrusively stood between Florena and real danger. They were together, they took care of each other, and that was all they wanted.

Joseph went with the Union army that slogged down the Mississippi Valley through the rain and mud of autumn and winter. Early in 1864 General Sherman began his advance toward Atlanta. The Confederates fought a desperate delaying action. In the bitter fighting in northern Georgia, Southern troops captured Joseph and Florena. They were sent to the dreaded prison camp south of Atlanta at Andersonville.

The camp was a nightmare. Too many men, too few tents. Open to rain, wind, and ice. No clean water. Almost no food. Prisoners died by the dozens every day.

Then in September 1864, Atlanta burned. To prevent their liberation by Sherman's army, the Confederates moved thousands of prisoners from Andersonville. A large group, including Joseph and Florena, were ordered to the rail town of Florence, South Carolina. They tramped along the King's Highway, past Savannah, toward Charleston. Many prisoners were too sick to go on, and had to be left behind. Joseph and Florena, aided by each other, were stronger than most and kept going.

The prisoners shivered in the cold rain, and grew numb from weakness and fatigue. At night the lucky ones found a bush or haystack to bed under, while the rest slept in open fields. The guards gave the prisoners what food they could find, but the desolated South had little to offer.

One night Joseph went to comfort one of his men, who lay dying. Later he couldn't find Florena, and went looking for her through the dark field. A guard saw Joseph in the field and thought he was trying to escape. He fired.

In the first light of morning, Florena found Joseph's body.

The other prisoners were so weak, they couldn't recognize a wife's grief.

In the hours and days that followed, Florena stumbled along blindly. She caught a deep cold which, combined with her grief, finally caused her to faint beside the road. She lapsed into a coma.

Instead of leaving her to die, someone took pity and tossed Florena into one of the wagons. The survivors of the long march reached Florence, only to learn that Sherman had captured Savannah, and now had his sights on South Carolina. Prisoners and guards alike were weary and sick.

As many as 16,000 Union prisoners were crowded into the small Florence stockade during the five months the camp operated. The crowded conditions and poor sanitation caused terrible epidemics, including the dreaded typhoid fever. Hundreds died every day.

Wagonloads of bodies were buried hastily in mass graves, shoulder to shoulder, with only blankets to cover the bodies. Records show that 2,802 Union soldiers died in the Florence camp. Many had no identification. The burial site became the Florence National Cemetery.

The people of Florence helped the prisoners with the little food and medicine they had. One doctor who treated a comatose patient was startled to discover that under the muddy, ragged uniform, the soldier was a woman. He called on the women of Florence to help. They brought clothes and nursed Florena until she regained consciousness. A daughter of one of the ladies brought a bowl of chrysanthemums, which reminded Florena of Pennsylvania and home.

For a while Florena helped nurse the other prisoners, but in January 1865 she fell ill with the fever and pneumonia. In her weakened state, she couldn't recover. Florena died on January

25. A few weeks later all sick prisoners were sent north by train.

The ladies of Florence prepared Florena for burial and dressed her in appropriate clothes. They called her "the soldier in skirts." The captain's orderly was laid to rest as a soldier of the United States Army. Her tombstone bore her real name, as well as the number 2480 and the date of her death.

Other facts of Florena's life are unknown. Her grave marker stands in the center of a large square, seemingly vacant, just inside the gates of Florence National Cemetery. If you look closely, you'll discover that she was buried in the center of hundreds of unknown soldiers.

Courtesy of J. K. Floyd

16

COMING HOME IN 1865

Private J. M. Lowrimore of Company F, 7th South Carolina Cavalry, surrendered at Appomattox Courthouse along with the rest of Robert E. Lee's Army of Northern Virginia. The American Civil War was about to end. Historians know civil wars end with the victors executing the captured losers, while the ones who escape flee into the mountains to carry on a guerrilla war that lasts for years. America's bloodiest time ended differently.

Robert E. Lee refused to continue the war on a guerrilla basis. The other Confederate commanders followed his example. Ulysses S. Grant's Union Army of the Potomac, gracious in victory, saluted the Confederate soldiers who stacked their arms at Appomattox. The Confederates returned the honor.

Still the nation suffered deep wounds. Abraham Lincoln's assassination opened the door to the period known as Reconstruction, a time of economic devastation for most Southerners. Private Lowrimore didn't know what was to come after Appomattox. All he knew was that he could finally go home.

Southern Historical Papers, Volume XV, lists Private Lowrimore as one of the soldiers paroled immediately after the surrender.

The Union army also allowed him to keep his horse. He began the long trip home to Bucksport, near Conway. He longed to see the black waters of the Waccamaw River, flowing near the farm where he grew up. Maybe the river could soak up some of his tiredness, or the pain and despair from the war. He aimed to try it.

Neither he nor his horse had anything to eat. The horse fell over dead near Goldsboro, North Carolina, so Private Lowrimore started walking. Somewhere along the way he lost one of his broken shoes, realized it when the thorns and rocks hurt him. He wrapped rags around his foot.

The days since he'd left Virginia blurred in his mind. His hunger hurt so badly for so long that it finally felt like food didn't even matter anymore. At night he sheltered himself the best he could under thickets and bushes, so his exhausted body could fall into a few hours of fitful sleep. His need to get home burned ever hotter.

Lowrimore was thirty-three years old when he staggered into Bucksport, but he was already an old man. He and his four brothers had answered the call to enlist in the Confederate Army early in 1862. Two of his brothers died in the fierce fighting in Virginia. For the rest of his life, people respectfully called Lowrimore "Mr. Jimsey."

The stories of his experiences, told by Mr. Jimsey to his children and grandchildren, passed into family history.

On the other side of Horry County, in Floyd's Township, Private Avery Floyd also returned home. He had enlisted in

Company B, Tucker's Cavalry. Those who survived fighting in Tucker's group later became Company F, 7th South Carolina Cavalry. Floyd and his nine brothers were the sons of J. R. Floyd, who was also called "Mr. Jimsey." Five of those sons died in battle, fighting for the Confederacy.

With all the loss in his family, it was a sad homecoming for Private Avery Floyd. Resolutely he set himself to the task of helping his parents and others get by in the aftermath of the war. He became a county leader. His wife, Penelope Williams Floyd, organized the first school in the Floyd's community. They also helped organize and build Floyd's Methodist Church.

"Arrival of a Federal Column at a Planter's House in Dixie"
from *Harper's Weekly,* 4 April, 1863
Courtesy of the N.C. Division of Archives and History

Sergeant Jeremiah Smith also appears on the roster of those who served in Company F, 7th South Carolina Cavalry. He lived in Socastee, Horry District. C. Foster Smith, in his 1993 book, *Jeremiah Smith and the Confederate War*, says of his grandfather:

"He might speak of danger or hunger or bravery or triumph as he sat with his family before a crackling log fire on a winter evening. But (in public) he chose to state his war record in three terse phrases: Volunteered for Confederate service in 1861, wounded near Richmond 1864, paroled at Appomattox 1865."

In later years Jeremiah Smith entered state politics. He served four years in the South Carolina House of Representatives and in various other offices. He was the last Confederate veteran to serve in the state senate. His election to his third term in the senate came when he was eighty years old.

These and all the other paroled soldiers of the Confederacy found defeat left a bitter taste. Yet they brought home the same courage and determination they had fought the war with to rebuild and restore their devastated South.

Those men lucky enough to survive, and to come home whole, had still lost years of their lives. Everything had changed when they returned: friends and relatives dead, farms abandoned, and people in desperate need. Nearly all the women wore black, mourning their dead husbands, brothers, fathers, or sons. The women had struggled those war years to meet the needs of their families. In some communities, women and girls had set up spinning wheels and looms in a school or barn or church. They gathered what they needed to spin and weave "linsey-woolsey" and rough cotton material, or to piece quilts. Everyone worked, regardless of age, trying to survive.

General William T. Sherman's Union army had left Georgia early in 1865 and marched through South Carolina, virtually unopposed. They left a path of destruction. After entering North Carolina, one of Sherman's soldiers said of South Carolina, "She has had an awful punishment."

Now the war was over, but it would still be long years before the desperate struggles to survive eased.

Interest rates in South Carolina rose to thirty-five percent. Congress raised tariffs on some factory machinery needed in the South to forty percent. Of the one hundred million dollars authorized for national public works from 1865 until 1875, the South received less than ten percent. Union occupation troops patrolled South Carolina until 1877.

Yet the end of the war also meant modern changes were on the way. The returning veterans had been "outside." They had seen and heard things the people at home knew nothing about. They had seen factory-made products and new inventions. They had ridden on trains, which no one saw in Horry County until 1887. New crops and fertilizers changed the idea of subsistence farming. Some of the veterans found their stories of new technologies doubted by those who had stayed at home. No wonder a few of them decided to migrate west and start a new life.

Horry County had suffered less than many other parts of the South. Being a sparsely populated area, it wasn't directly in Sherman's line of march. The county had never really depended on slave labor, so many farms continued self-supporting. The people were independent, used to no help from the outside. The worst problem was the rising taxes.

Some outsiders moved in from across the rivers, abandoning their debt-ridden land for a small farm they could buy or share-crop. These people found more opportunities in the isolated county. Everyone's attention focused on surviving, on fighting the overwhelming poverty, and on making a living.

In 1872 the United States Congress passed the General Amnesty Act, which pardoned all former Confederates except top ranking officials. Southerners had their right to vote reinstated. The election of 1876 was a revolt against Reconstruction.

Almost an entire generation had missed the chance to get an education, unless mothers could teach their children. When a few schools finally opened, some parents were eager to learn along with their children.

Northerners called it "The War of Southern Rebellion." Southerners called it "The War of Northern Aggression." The bitter Civil War pitted friend against friend, brother against brother. But in 1865 the fighting had finally ended, and it was time for a little optimism. The parolees from Appomattox and the other surrender sites, and the prisoners who straggled out of the Northern POW camps were all worn-out, but they came home as quickly as they could. It was time to make a new life.

17

THE GHOSTS OF OLD GUNN CHURCH

Anyone who has visited Old Gunn Church is reluctant to return, especially at Halloween or on any dark night.

The old church ruins attracts visitors, and leaves an impression. Its name was Prince Frederick's Episcopal Church, Pee Dee, but it is better known as Old Gunn, named for the architect who fell to his death from the steep roof.

Only the massive, crumbling bell tower remains of the once lovely Gothic structure, located on Plantersville Road, off Highway 701 between Conway and Georgetown. Encroaching pines and white grave markers form a background, making the tower look like a lonely keep, a watchtower guarding the entrance to a great English estate. The once elaborate house of worship had stood empty and abandoned for long years; its pews and furnishings were gone; stormy winds and rain blew through broken windows and doors. Then the building burned.

Plantersville Road was named for the rich plantations, which stretched for miles along the banks of the Pee Dee and Black Rivers. The community of planters was the center of Prince Frederick's Parish, established in 1734. In 1859 a new church was commissioned for the Episcopalian "rice barons," a wealthy close-knit society. Only the finest materials were to be used in the construction. Most came from England. Unfortunately the Union coastal blockade during the Civil War halted the delivery of the imports.

Even without the rest of the expensive materials, the construction of the church went on. Workers used materials from nearby. Residents came to watch the work. The stately and majestic structure promised to be the most beautiful building ever seen. The Gothic bell tower took shape and rose above the treetops into the sky.

In one instant all the promise turned black. Mr. Gunn, the chief architect, was up on the slick tiled roof, directing some workers, when his foot slipped out from under him. The workers and spectators all heard his scream as he plummeted to the ground.

After Gunn's death, work on the bell tower came to a halt. Many workers refused to return. They insisted the place was haunted. The unfinished church was abandoned.

The structure sat empty through the war and the decade that followed. There was no money for materials. As the planters saw their distinctive way of life disappear, some of the old plantations had to be sold and divided. People began to move away.

Northern investors bought some of the old properties. Some prosperity slowly returned. Other churches saw the promise of the unfinished structure and donated money to complete construction. When the work was completed in 1877, Prince Frederick's Episcopal drew many worshippers. They formed a fine choir. The members came to practice at dusk almost every night. Strains of organ music lifted on the winds that stirred the trees, touching the ears of the travelers who stopped their carriages along the road to listen.

Some say the choir still sings today. Some people have heard the sounds of organ and voices mingling with the wind and night sounds of the deserted church yard.

As the times changed in the late 1800s, the depressed postwar

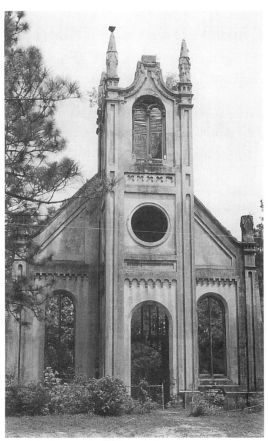

The ruins of Old Gunn Church
Courtesy of Barry McGee

economy worsened. Members moved to Georgetown or Charleston to find jobs. People sold or abandoned homes. As the congregation dwindled, services went from regular to occasional, then only on special dates, and finally ceased.

With the telling of the tales, the building came to be known as Old Gunn Church. Its real name and history have almost been forgotten.

Over the years various people have reported strange and unexplained occurrences at the church. In the upper tower, which is inaccessible, many have seen lights. Others have heard noises ranging from singing to moaning and shrieking. Worst of all, sometimes the silence is pierced by the deathly scream of Mr. Gunn.

Each year at Halloween, carloads of young people make a pilgrimage to Old Gunn Church for the sole purpose of being frightened. The ancient encircling graveyard, the swaying trees, the ragged bushes and tall grasses frame a haunting scene.

The rubble of the burned church has been cleared away, and only the bell tower remains. A locked fence encloses the church ruins and cemetery, but visitors can stand nearby to watch and listen. Once in a while a funeral is held in the cemetery, and families continue to take care of the grounds.

In the darkness of night, with wispy fog obscuring the pale moon, any noise sounds ghostly. Leaves crackle, birds shriek, and the wind keens in the high tree limbs. Tombstones gleam. It is a scene ripe for a haunting. Generation after generation gets haunted at Old Gunn Church.

18

SANDY ISLAND

A PLACE CALLED HOME

Sandy Island isn't as flat as most land at the coast. Tidal waters, thousands of years ago, caused the Great Pee Dee River to deposit sand hills near the center of the island, creating the highest point in Georgetown County. Much of the surrounding land is swampy, and covered with moss-laden oaks and thickets of pine trees. Creamy white sand contrasts with the bright shades of green.

Located a few miles off the King's Highway, south of Brookgreen Gardens, Sandy Island can be reached only by boat. Its boundaries are the Waccamaw River on the east, the Pee Dee River on the west, Bull Creek on the north, and Thoroughfare Creek on the south. The 13,000-acre island is now home to about thirty-five families.

Soon after the settlement of Charleston in 1670, rice became an important crop, thanks to Henry Woodward. England and Europe were "rice-hungry," and Carolina Waccamaw Gold Rice was the best in the world. Seven planters claimed rice fields on

Sandy Island. Many of the working slaves made their homes on the island.

Everything changed with the Civil War. The newly freed slaves heard rumor after rumor, and felt they could trust no one. Some said the Yankee soldiers would capture them and ship them north, away from their families and homes. Others said their former owners weren't about to let them remain free. In the midst of so much turbulence, where should the former slaves go? What should they do?

They wisely decided to stay where they were. They learned the importance of a paper that showed ownership and gave them the right to stay. For a handful of former slaves, Sandy Island became a true sanctuary.

One of them, Phillip Washington, bought Mount Arena Plantation soon after the Civil War's end. The group settled together there. Other former slaves who had no place to go joined them on the island.

At first the group hunted, fished, and farmed, living a primitive existence. As they became more confident, they began to trade for necessities with Eason's Store in Murrells Inlet, or across the Pee Dee in Plantersville. Some of the former slaves took jobs across the rivers. By the 1930s, Brookgreen Gardens offered employment; others worked in the mills in Georgetown. Sandy Island was always the home they returned to.

Health care was always a problem. Mosquitoes breeding in the low marshes spread "Swamp Fever" (Malaris). Before the Civil War, the families of planters had spent the hot humid months of summer at the beaches or in the mountains. When the planters returned in the fall, their first question was always, "How many died?" The former slaves still faced the problem, and fought the disease valiantly over the years.

Children started crossing the river to attend school, riding school boats and buses. Electricity came to Sandy Island in the 1960s. Many changes have come, but island life is still secluded and secure.

On March 7, 1997, Sandy Island was officially dedicated as a Public Trust Nature preserve, with 95 percent of the island undeveloped. Fifteen state and federal agencies, private businesses, conservation groups, and many individuals had worked together for years to preserve the island with respect to its natural state. At the ceremony, a barred owl and a cooper's hawk were released as symbols of the sanctuary. Lindsay Pettus, board member of the Nature Conservancy, said, "This is South Carolina's Garden of Eden."

Natural treasures on Sandy Island include a lovely lagoon, called Indian Lake, and many rare plants and endangered birds. Perhaps the most important treasure is the heritage of the island's hearty inhabitants. Their timeless sense of worth, pride in the past, and hope for the future keep Sandy Island their beloved place called home.

19

THE DUTCHMAN

OF MEDWAY PLANTATION

For more than three centuries, Medway House has stood on a slight rise facing the Back River, a wide creek that flows into the Cooper River. Surrounded by green lawns and plantings, the lovely old house is sheltered by huge moss-draped oaks. The house's mellow, rosy bricks were made and dried on the site, then stuccoed. Located on a country road near Goose Creek, not far from Charleston, Medway is the oldest brick house still standing in South Carolina.

Most of the old plantations have their own ghost stories. Medway outdoes the others with three spectral figures in permanent residence. This is the story of one of them.

* * *

During that special time of day on southern plantations, when each passing minute deepens the fresh darkness, the sights and sounds of nearby cities are far away. A gentle solitude settles over the land. In an upstairs bedroom of Medway House, there is an old brick fireplace. The blaze is the only light in the room.

Shadows flicker.

A short, stocky gentleman sits in a heavy wooden armchair, gazing into the smoldering flames. His clothing is the style worn in the 1600s in Holland or France. He wears a tall, broad-brimmed hat, set with a silver buckle in its band. His jacket, fashioned of rich green material, features a wide snug collar and cuffs. Knee-length pants, stockings, and polished buckled shoes complete his outfit.

Firelight reflects off the man's silver buttons and buckles. His hands cup a cherished pipe. His plump, bearded face is complacent and satisfied.

The door opens. A guest who will sleep in the upstairs bedroom enters. The gentleman looks around, then slowly vanishes. The fire flickers before the guest, and the chair remains, but the man is gone, leaving the guest wondering if he really saw him.

Occasionally a guest sleeping in this bedroom awakens to catch a glimpse of the man enjoying his pipe before the fire, just before he vanishes.

The man in the chair, Jan Van Arrsens, Seigneur de Weirnhoudt, was a wealthy Dutch nobleman who immigrated to Carolina in 1686. His beautiful wife, Sabina de Vignon, and a party of friends and servants came with him, all seeking their fortunes in the New World.

Van Arrsens secured a land grant on the scenic Back River, and began planning for his home. Records of the early period are incomplete, but he apparently received a grant of 2,100 acres from the Lords Proprietors in 1686. Van Arrsens called his estate "Medway," for the Medway River in Trent, England, where the Dutch had won a sea victory.

The Dutchman planned a home to rival those he remembered in Europe. The central section to the house had stairstep gables that encouraged evil spirits to walk down them, instead of invading the rooms. The bedroom where the Dutchman sits is located in this section.

Unfortunately, with the building scarcely underway, Van Arrsens died. His grave had no permanent marker, and cannot now be found. His lovely young wife Sabina was extremely rich and soon married Thomas Smith, a land owner with the title of Landgrave.

Thomas Smith probably completed Medway House. Again the records are hazy, but Sabina knew well what her first husband had planned.

The couple enjoyed a pleasant plantation life. In May 1693, Thomas Smith was appointed Proprietary Governor of South Carolina, and served capably until his death on November 16, 1694. Sabina had to sadly bury her second husband at Medway. She marked Smith's grave with a stone slab and a low brick wall; it is the only marked grave of a proprietary governor located in the state.

Sabina's first husband, Van Arrsens, never left Medway. His ghost began to appear in his room soon after his death. Apparently his wife's remarriage didn't upset him. Perhaps he liked the love and care taken of his home, and the improvements and additions. Everyone who has felt the ghost's presence has noticed his air of contentment as he sits by the fire with his pipe.

Medway Plantation had several different owners its first two hundred years. Lumbering and rice cultivation brought riches to the owners before the Civil War. Peter Gaillard Stoney bought Medway in 1835, and his family owned it for the next ninety-four years. They added the west wing and planted the two avenues of live oaks. The earthquake of 1886 caused the stepped gables to crumble, but the Stoneys had them restored.

By the winter of 1929, the house was an abandoned ruin. Hunters sometimes used it for a shelter. Gertrude and Sidney Legendre saw the avenue of oaks, the tangle of vines and shrubbery, and the pale pink bricks of the aging manor house, and with youthful enthusiasm, decided to buy it. In 1930 they purchased Medway, Spring Grove, Pine Grove, and other pieces of land that totaled 8,600 acres.

The restoration and modernization of the beautiful Medway House made a comfortable and livable home for the Legendre family. The careful design of the grounds and formal garden complements the buildings. The Medway Environmental Trust preserves and protects the pine-hardwood habitat as a refuge for many endangered species of birds and animals. The estate is a special place for the family, and for the state of South Carolina.

The Dutchman has much to smile about these days, as he sits in his favorite room. The fire flickers and he smokes his treasured pipe, approving the changes and the care given his home. It's not a bad way to pass the years.

20

THE HAUNTING OF LITCHFIELD MANOR

The sound of the bell ringing at the Litchfield Plantation gate meant that someone wished to be admitted. No one was there. Night after night came the eerie ringing. The ominous sound continued until the owners finally had to remove the bell.

* * *

Litchfield Plantation, once the center of a rich rice kingdom, lies along the Waccamaw River west of the King's Highway. The Simons family of Litchfield, England settled on a 2,000-acre land grant in the early 1700s. The house was built around 1740. The estate was divided in 1794, one half called Willbrook Plantation staying in the Simons family, while the Litchfield half was sold. The new owners were the Tuckers from Georgetown, newly arrived from Bermuda.

The Tuckers developed a fine system of flooding and draining their rice fields. By 1850 the plantation produced one million pounds of rice per year. Freighters sailed up the Waccamaw to Litchfield landing to carry cargoes of rice to European markets. The Tuckers amassed a tremendous fortune.

97

Henry Massingberd Tucker, born in 1831, trained as a doctor to meet the needs of his large family and great number of slaves. He served with the Confederate army in the Civil War until the surrender at Appomattox. He returned home, determined to keep his beloved plantation. Many of his former slaves stayed on to live and work in the only place they knew. Tucker resolved to serve them, his family, friends, and community in every way possible.

As the closest doctor to all the great plantations of Waccamaw Neck, Tucker faced numerous emergencies: accidents, strokes, heart attacks, and severe illnesses. Most of his patients had no money, but Tucker never turned anyone down. His consideration for all those who needed him was well known.

Often the doctor received calls at night to treat someone. After he rode out on his great bay horse, a faithful servant who lived in a small cabin nearby closed the plantation gate, then locked and barred it. When the doctor returned, a light tap on the bell woke the servant who opened the gate.

Eventually the servant took a fancy to a young woman on an adjoining plantation. Keeping it from the doctor, the servant married her. Often he slipped away at night to visit her, so when the doctor rode up, cold and tired, no one opened the gate. As he grew more frustrated, the doctor would bang on the bell with his silver riding crop. Usually he rapped so loudly that someone else would wake and come let him in. Other times the doctor had to tie his horse, climb the wall, and walk down the long avenue to his home. Those times he used a small staircase in the back of the house so as not to disturb his family.

Dr. Tucker died in 1904, the last member of his family to own Litchfield Plantation. He was buried in Georgetown. The days of the great rice fortunes had ended, but some say the doctor loved his rice kingdom so much that his spirit remained there.

The gate at Litchfield Plantation
Courtesy of Barry McGee

Shortly after the doctor's death, one foggy night the gatehouse bell rang. With no one there. The eerie ring came on other nights, always late, just as if the doctor had returned from a call. Successive owners of the plantation heard the bell.

Residents of the house have caught a glimpse of a white-haired gentleman slowly climbing the back stairs to the bedroom. When people approach him, the man vanishes.

Others have seen on dark, foggy nights a horse and rider on

King's Road. The pair lingers near the Litchfield gate.

Litchfield Plantation is such a beautiful and pleasant place, who could blame Henry Tucker for not wanting to leave? The gracious ante-bellum home has been refurbished and restored to the elegance of more romantic days. The wrought iron gates, set in old brick walls, open to a quarter-mile avenue leading to the house. Giant live oaks draped with silvery streamers of moss, spread their limbs overhead to create a dusky corridor. Brilliant azaleas, blooming in season, enhance the beauty of the drive and house.

So on dark, overcast nights, when moisture drips from the moss, don't be surprised if at Litchfield the breeze carries the sound of a faint tinkle of a bell. It might be the good doctor returning.

21

PRESIDENTIAL VISITORS

It was a frightening moment for the small group. There was no time to spare in such an emergency; the guides remembered tragedies caused by the quicksand. The group worked with poles and ropes to free the unfortunate one trapped in a pit. This victim was none other than president of the United States, Grover Cleveland.

President Cleveland had a friend, former Confederate General Edward Alexander, who owned property along Winyah Bay, near Georgetown. The general loved to tell stories of the glories of duck hunting in old abandoned rice fields along the coast. So Cleveland had planned a brief trip south for rest and relaxation. Early in December 1894, the president and his party sailed into Winyah Bay for five days of hunting.

While walking around on South Island, the president had mistakenly landed in a mire pit, which held him fast. He was a short, portly man, too heavy to be pulled out easily. Yet he had a calm manner, which proved to help greatly in the urgent proceedings to free him. He didn't panic, but simply waited and followed directions, hefting his weight as he was told.

In later years, members of the group that helped President Cleveland loved to tell how they had saved his life, or about how they'd told the president what to do, "and he did it."

Stuck in the mire and quicksand, suction continued to pull the president down. The panting men finally freed him, but not without leaving behind his heavy hunting boots. They carried Cleveland to higher ground.

In spite of the quicksand episode, the press sent back glowing reports of the president's visit to northern newspapers. They described the hunting, the fishing, and the matchless beauty of the area. The reports encouraged others to come south. Wealthy

President and Mrs. Grover Cleveland take a morning stroll;
from *Frank Leslie's Illustrated Newspaper*, 19 May, 1888
Courtesy of the N.C. Division of Archives and History

Northerners visited and bought some of the abandoned plantations. Local people called this development "the second Yankee invasion."

The original presidential visit to the Grand Strand took place in 1791. First President George Washington made a goodwill tour of the South. As a former surveyor, he wanted to get a feel for the extent of the nation and the "look" of the land. He also wanted to show appreciation for supporters of the Constitution, and reconcile those who had opposed it.

President Washington recorded in his diary that he traveled the King's Highway south from Wilmington, by way of Little River, Gause's Swash, and Singleton and Wither's Swashes (in Myrtle Beach). He described the Grand Strand as "...sand and piney barrens...with very few inhabitants..."

The entourage made its way to Georgetown on April 30, 1791. The entry in the president's diary reads: "We crossed the Waggamaw to Georgetown by descending the river three miles..." He mentioned that all the rivers seemed to be at flood stage, a common occurrence in April.

The citizens provided the president and his party royal entertainment in Georgetown and later in Charleston. Washington especially enjoyed a tea party attended by "upwards of fifty ladies who had assembled on the occasion." His party left Georgetown at six o'clock the next morning in order to enjoy breakfast (brunch) at beautiful Hampton Plantation. The hosts were Harriott Horry and her mother, Eliza Lucas Pinckney.

In 1824 another president traveled down the King's Highway

22 ⬧ 5

CLIFTON PLANTATION

President George Washington on his
southern tour traveled southward
over this road, April 27-30, 1791.
While in this vicinity the day and
night of April 29, he was the
guest of Captain William Alston
on this plantation, Clifton,
which originally was a
part of the Hobcaw Barony.

Courtesy of J. K. Floyd

to see the land and the people. James Monroe, president from 1817 to 1825, endured little criticism or opposition. He was so popular that his terms were later called "the era of good feeling."

Monroe's party journeyed south from Wilmington in carriages and on horseback, following the highway along the Grand Strand. In Georgetown, Charleston, and wherever he visited, great crowds gathered to see and cheer the president.

Over a century later, another visitor came to coastal Carolina.

President Franklin D. Roosevelt was a very tired, sick man. Hoping to rest and recuperate, Roosevelt arrived at Waccamaw Neck as the guest of Bernard Baruch, owner of the huge estate called Hobcaw Barony.

With World War II blazing, Roosevelt's visit had to be kept

President James Monroe
Courtesy of the N.C. Division of Archives and History

top-secret. However residents of Georgetown and the coast knew something was going on. Coast Guard ships patrolled Winyah Bay and the entrance to the ocean. Planes droned overhead. Uniformed marines clustered around the entrance to Hobcaw Barony. Armed Secret Service agents stood vigilantly around and inside Hobcaw House. Obviously something unusual was afoot.

By 1944 Roosevelt suffered from fatigue and stress, along with hypertension and heart disease. Years of depression and war had strained him to the breaking point. He badly needed to rest.

At the same time, the president had to stay aware of world events. He worked as much as his doctor would allow. He did a little fishing in the creeks and river mouth, in places where he could be ferried in his wheelchair. Polio had paralyzed his legs in 1921, when he was 39 years old. This never stopped his political career.

During his month's stay at Hobcaw, Roosevelt found time to take a brief trip north to Myrtle Beach. Without fanfare or publicity, he visited the hospital at Myrtle Beach Air Field. With his aides and wheelchair, the president toured the small facility and talked to some patients and hospital orderlies. He noted that some of the orderlies were Germans from the Myrtle Beach Prisoner of War Camp. Some prisoners had helped construct the air field; others had duty in the hospital or other places.

The president had few visitors during his restful stay. First Lady Eleanor Roosevelt and their daughter came for a brief visit. General Mark Clark brought a report on the coming invasion of Europe. The prime minister of Australia arrived to discuss the war in the Pacific.

In May the president returned to Washington. It seemed too soon, but he was in better health and spirits. When he talked with reporters, his famous smile beamed from a suntanned face. He plunged into the work at hand.

Unfortunately, President Roosevelt died less than a year later, in April 1945, just as the war in Europe was about to end.

22

THE OLD ARKE

Hurricane winds and piercing rain couldn't knock the house down. Even when nature had flattened or washed away every other building around, "the Arke" earned its nickname the hard way; it survived storm after storm for a century and a half.

Located at what is now called Surfside Beach, the Old Arke was six miles south of Myrtle Beach, along the King's Highway.

The *1820 Atlas of South Carolina* by Robert Mills mentioned the Arke Plantation as the home of John Tillman. Horry County recorded a survey of Tillman's plantation as: "Resurvey of an 1838 Map, 3,194 acres, 1-1/2 miles ocean front and stretching 3 miles inland." The map clearly showed the house (The Old Arke), outbuildings, and cleared fields. No deed to the property was ever recorded, but the land could have been a Royal grant to the Tillman family before the American Revolution.

Tillman's plantation home, like many others, was a "four-square" house—four rooms on both the upstairs and downstairs levels. It was a stark, bare house built with no pretense of beauty or ornamentation, with unpainted, weathered, gray siding. Its picture would never be in a book of classic southern mansions.

Yet it was built to withstand summer storms and winter gales, frigid cold and sweltering heat, as a haven of safety for all those who sheltered there. It survived the worst storms from the 1800s until the 1950s.

In 1822 one of the worst storms ever recorded struck Pawleys Island and along the Grand Strand. The loss of life and property was staggering. The wind wrenched homes from their foundations and splintered them. One of South Carolina's favorite ghosts first appeared just prior to this storm, The Gray Man of Pawleys Island. He warned a family to leave the island, saving their lives. Residents have spotted him before practically every storm since. If you see The Gray Man, head inland.

The Old Arke withstood the 1822 hurricane, unlike its neighbors. After that, as other storms approached, people took refuge there. Extra stocks of cured meat and cornmeal were always on hand.

In 1893 two storms devastated the coast. The "Great Storm" late in August alone caused the loss of a thousand ships, and untold numbers of lives. Before the damage could be repaired, another storm and tidal wave struck in October, washing away buildings and landmarks. Again the loss of lives was great.

During these storms, fishermen along Surfside Beach saved their lives by hurrying to the Old Arke. The tidal waters smashed inland, inundating houses, crops, livestock, and people, yet the Arke withstood the force. When water swept into the house, the fishermen chopped a hole in the floor to let it flow through. And they survived.

After the storm died and the flood waters receded, rescue workers stared in disbelief at the damage. They found the Old Arke was just about the only building still standing from Murrells Inlet to Wilmington, North Carolina.

Records state that in 1850 wealthy John Tillman owned 57 slaves. His main crops were rice and potatoes. Tillman died in 1865, near the end of the Civil War, having lost his wealth and property. The Old Arke Plantation was divided and sold. Most of the property went to the Roach family. Gradually people began calling the area "Roach's Beach," and continued to do so for the next fifty years.

In the 1920s, George J. Holliday, of Gallivant's Ferry on the Pee Dee River, bought Roach's property. He renamed it "Floral Beach" for his wife and daughter. He began to develop the beach, first building a large cottage, Holliday House, for his family and their guests. Dr. V. F. Platt from Conway also bought land. Other people came.

The Old Arke, then well over a century old, wasn't forgotten. Holliday added twenty new rooms, a wide front, and side porches to the building, changing it to a fine hotel for Floral Beach. Workers served delicious meals there. Families came for vacation and dinner. The Old Arke had a new look and a new life, at least for a while.

By the 1950s, many other tourist homes and small motels had sprung up. The old hotel was no longer needed. By the middle of the decade it stood abandoned and decaying on the site at 3rd Avenue South and Willow Street. People began to take away souvenirs—a board, a door, a piece of molding. This was the death knell of the Old Arke. Though storms could never destroy the building, workers quickly dismantled it. The King's Highway and the Grand Strand lost another landmark.

Floral Beach changed its name to Surfside Beach in the 1950s. It has grown considerably since then, but hopefully it will retain its image as a family beach, the safe haven it's been since the days of the Old Arke.

23

A WHALE OF A TALE

There wasn't much excitement or activity at the beach in 1900. Construction of the first big hotel, the Seaside Inn, had begun. Other buildings would follow. The few hardy souls who stayed at the beach overnight pitched tents or rigged up a covered wagon for a place to sleep. Swarms of mosquitoes and sand fleas were delighted to see them.

Those who planned to eat at the beach brought food with them, and hoped to catch a few fish to fry. Leftovers attracted roving animals and hovering sea gulls. All in all, it was scarcely a vacation to write home about.

The Grand Strand was a treasure still waiting to be discovered. Myrtle Beach was called New Town, for lack of a better name.

Then someone reported that the huge carcass of a whale had washed ashore at Hurl Rocks (20th Avenue South). Most people in Horry County were acquainted with only one whale, the one that swallowed Jonah in the Bible. People said the one on the beach was too big to believe. Everyone had to check it out.

The railroad from Conway had been completed as far as the big Pine Island lumber mill. The train operated mainly to transport building materials and equipment for laying more tracks. It was surely not intended for passengers. However, in view of the unusual circumstances, the crew tried to meet the demand. They placed cross ties along the sides of flat cars, and laid boards across for seats. Fearful souls found it an unsafe arrangement, to be out there while hurtling along at fifteen or twenty miles per hour. Most people decided that the opportunity to see a whale meant they should take their chances on the train.

The crowds gathered early in Conway along the Waccamaw River for the ferry across to the train. Since it was mostly a party, everyone took picnic baskets full of goodies to share. Ladies

The Conway and Seashore Train near the turn of the century
Used by permission of the Horry County Museum

carried umbrellas and wore long-skirted dresses and wide-brimmed straw hats, tied under their chins. People crowded onto the train.

The wood-burning engine, the "Black Maria," puffed and spouted clouds of black smoke filled with bits of charred wood and live cinders. Grass and woods along the tracks kept catching on fire. Each time the crew jumped off the train and beat out the flames. Many realized the real hazard wasn't falling from the speeding train, but the fire catching on the umbrellas, straw hats, and stylish dresses.

The train finally arrived at Pine Island and the passengers clamored off. Wagons carried a few the rest of the way, but most of the crowd walked the mile and a half to Hurl Rocks. They talked of seeing "Jonah's Whale," and the details they'd be able to add to the Sunday School lesson on Jonah.

At the beach they came across the vast beast, lying on the sand. It's body stood twice as high as any grown man. They walked around it, staring at its huge tail, wondering how anything so large could live. Some looked right into its big eye, and through its teeth. Everyone oohed and aahed.

Then the ladies spread their lunches and social hour began. Many walked down the beach and collected shells as momentoes.

Before any of them were ready, it was time to walk back to Pine Island for the return trip. The crew had loaded enough resinous pine logs for fuel, insuring more black smoke and sparks on the way home. Everyone had holes burned in their clothing and umbrellas, but they all agreed it had been well worth it to see

The whale at Myrtle Beach
Used by permission of the Horry County Museum

the whale.

Others made the journey over the next few days, so that by the time a group of whalers arrived, everyone wanted to get rid of the carcass. The whalers had harpooned the mammoth leviathan earlier, but had to cut it loose from their ship because of a violent storm. Now they went to work. They stripped away the meat, blubber, and skin, leaving the bony structure for the sea gulls to pick clean.

People traveled to the beach to measure and count the ribs. Children worked up the courage to climb on top of the bones to play.

The big skeleton turned out to be more interesting than the whale.

24

THE FIRST PAVILION AT MYRTLE BEACH

Travelers on the present-day King's Highway often have Myrtle Beach as their destination. Even though they have hundreds of things to do at the beach, nearly all of them visit the pavilion.

In the early 1900s, there were no radios, movies, video games, rides, television, or scores of shops and restaurants at the beach. The few automobiles didn't want to hazard the rutted, sandy roads. Children entertained themselves with their imaginations. Then something exciting came along.

By 1901 the Conway and Seashore Railroad to New Town (Myrtle Beach) had been completed, and the big new hotel, the Seaside Inn, opened for business. The train's purpose was to transport logs and lumber products from the Pine Island Mill to Conway, but more and more people discovered the beach and rode the train to get there.

The Myrtle Beach Farms Company realized how popular the beach had become, and decided in 1908 to build a pavilion. It opened as a place of fun and excitement. Everyone found something wonderful and safe to do. From the first day, the pavilion

The first Myrtle Beach pavilion
Used by permission of the Horry County Museum

was a success. Connected to the big inn by a boardwalk, the pavilion served as a gathering place for summer visitors and the small number of year round residents.

One writer called it "the round dance pavilion." From a distance, it did look round, since it was built with many sides. Each side had an open window. Wooden shutters covered the openings in stormy weather and in winter. Blowing sand piled up on the porch surrounding the pavilion, and seeped into the inner room. Sweeping out the sand was a daily chore.

Like the Seaside Inn, the pavilion had a red roof and gray walls with white trim. A Delco system (a generator for electricity) supplied lights for both buildings. All the cottages used candles or oil lamps, which flared and smoked in the sea breezes. The bright electric lights stood out on the beach.

Someone donated a worn-out, squeaky, wind-up Victrola, with a small, morning glory shaped speaker on top. The people found about a dozen records to play. Some were hymns. The children thought it was "magic music!"

A visitor to the beach who brought a guitar or "fiddle" would probably be persuaded to furnish some live music. The young people practiced the waltz, the foxtrot, and when the parents weren't looking, the shimmy. The parents spent their time on the outside porch, talking, catching up on the news, and watching through the windows.

One summer the nightlife grew more exciting. Four or five college boys formed a band, and played all the latest songs. People traveled from all around to listen and dance. Some local boys sold soft drinks, roasted peanuts, and candy that were brought over on the train.

An evening at the pavilion meant everyone dressed up. They wore shoes and socks, since bare feet weren't accepted. Girls wore crisp, starched, organdy dresses, which made sunburned shoulders itch. Older girls wore long, soft voile dresses, colorful and pretty, as they danced with boys in white trousers and slicked-down hair. The Delco lights glowed off the young faces.

The evenings were magic. Each was too good to last forever. Sooner or later, the soft strains of "Good Night, Ladies" played, the signal to say goodnight and go home. The kids never wanted to leave. Parents reminded them they could come another night, but still the young ones complained. The adults cut off the lights, closed the doors and shutters, and propped the rockers against the walls so they wouldn't blow over.

Congregations used the pavilion on Sundays for worship services. The first church at Myrtle Beach wasn't built until 1921.

After years of fun, the little round pavilion grew unsafe. Countless storms had rocked it until it became ramshackled, so workmen tore it down in 1925. A larger, wooden building, built nearer the beach, replaced it. That one burned in 1944.

Myrtle Beach Farms designed and constructed an almost storm-proof pavilion, which opened in 1949. Its walls are reinforced concrete. The second floor dance hall and stage have served as a center for activities like the Sun-Fun Festival, and the Miss South Carolina Beauty Pageant. Today the pavilion's bright lights and loud noises draw thousands of visitors from all over the world.

Perhaps if you listen with your heart, and remember quieter times, you might imagine scratchy music from an old wind-up Victrola.

25

PROPER BEACH ATTIRE

Consider this important decision: would you prefer gray and white or blue and white bed ticking for your glamorous bathing suit?

The women and girls of 1902 wore bathing suits cut from mattress cover material, which was as heavy and stiff as canvas. The popular new style featured a high, snug neck band, long sleeves gathered at the wrists, and long, full gathered pants or divided skirt, tightly anchored at the ankles. Ladies all wore wide-brimmed straw hats, which tied under their chins.

Some suits had a skirt over the gathered pants. The skirt tended to float when the wearer waded out into the water. A bevy of women in the water looked like a bunch of open umbrellas, topped with mannequin figures in straw hats. When the heavy material got saturated with sea water, women could scarcely drag themselves up onto dry land.

"Going swimming" was quite a misnomer. The only thing the well-dressed women could do was wade in shallow water, hoping the waves wouldn't knock them over. Portly ladies always wore corsets under the heavy suits, and everyone wore rubber beach shoes. Then, after swimming, the costume made a cumbersome mass of material that needed washing and drying later.

Men wore long pants or denim overalls and shirt to venture out into the water. A few daring ones rolled up their pants' legs. That inevitably led to shorts.

This photo from about 1915 shows the first bath house at Myrtle Beach, where swimmers donned their stylish suits.
Used by permission of the Horry County Museum

By 1915 children were allowed to wear black woolen jersey bathing suits, with short sleeves and knee-length pants. Such suits gave kids more freedom of action as they ran and played, though they still took a long time to dry. Many children couldn't afford store-bought suits, and simply wore old clothes to wade and swim.

By the mid-1920s, beach attire had changed. Ladies shortened their skirts to knee length. Shirt tops or middy blouses, with shorter pants, topped a short full skirt, which was made of thinner, lighter materials.

A 1916 swimsuit, complete with shoes and parasol
Courtesy of the N.C. Division of Archives and History

Beach pajamas became popular in 1930. For those who just
wanted to lounge or stroll, these one-piece garments were made
of cotton and printed with bright, splashy tropical designs and
colors. Young people gladly abandoned the old gray and white
suits as relics of the Victorian Era. Older people shook their heads
and muttered about the "young ones going to the dogs."

An article in the July 31, 1935 *Myrtle Beach - Today and Tomorrow* said that men going shirtless was strictly forbidden at Myrtle and other public beaches. The trend was to wear boxer shorts or trunks with matching tops. The knee-length trunks were made of heavy material and belted at the waist. One beltless style came with an inner drawstring.

Three soldiers visit the beach in 1917
Courtesy of the N.C. Division of Archives and History

B. V. D. Co. surprised the country and caused favorable and unfavorable comments with shorter, better fitting trunks that quickly grew in popularity.

Also in the 1930s, "polo shirts" appeared. These heavy cotton knit shirts had a collar which was to stay securely buttoned.

Southern Bell Telephone Company employees
model gym costumes and a bathing suit in 1931
Courtesy of the N.C. Division of Archives and History

Comments at first were mostly that undershirts should not be worn in public. Opposition gradually lessened, and polo shirts appeared in bright colors, vivid stripes, and "unimaginable color combinations." Young people loved them. New styles included crew necks and V-necked shirts for casual wear.

Playing at Myrtle Beach
Used by permission of the Horry County Museum

Some young men wore lounging slacks for the beach. Though not suitable for working at jobs, these full, loose trousers complemented the colorful lounging pajamas worn by young ladies. To the magic music of the new "juke box," together they danced the night away. Light materials and styles were certainly welcome in the heat and humidity of summer.

Feet were liberated too. Sandals for men and women became popular beach wear in the 1930s, replacing heavier leather shoes. Open-work sandals and espadrilles used rope, cork, wood, or fabric, with leather or rubber soles. The new designs were light, comfortable, and appropriate for a vacation atmosphere.

There were no plastics or acrylic fibers, so designers worked with natural materials for attractive shoes and clothing. Most of the cloth was made of cotton, the South's commodity. Wool, linen, and the combination "linsey-woolsey" were also used. Natural silk, a precious and costly material from China, was used for more expensive clothing.

A style worn by some young men in the 1920s and 1930s didn't become very popular or last long. "Knickerbockers," better known as "Knickers" and sometimes called "Plus Fours," was a style of short, full, knee pants that was often worn for sports. You may still occasionally see "Golf Knickers."

In the 1930s, "Bikini" was the name of an atoll, a crescent-shaped group of tiny coral islands in the Pacific Ocean, two hundred miles south of Guam. No one suspected that someday a swimsuit would be called bikini. The style uses about a half yard of material for the bra top and skimpy pants. Bikinis have remained popular for generations.

The words from the old song may describe beach dress today: "Anything goes!" Create your own costume, from the simplest to the most bizarre, as long as the body is partly covered. There are no nude beaches at Myrtle Beach. Some outfits come close.

Customs and styles have changed greatly in the last hundred years. Who knows what people will wear a hundred years from now?

26

BEWARE THE RIPTIDE

As a beautiful summer's day in 1998 ended, a vacation came to a tragic end.

The shadows lengthened on the wide, white, sandy beach, while only a scattering of shore birds remained. The last curious onlookers had gone home. The lifeguards, Horry County Police, Surfside Police, and other personnel had done everything possible, but they couldn't work a miracle. The drowning victim had been taken to the hospital, there to be officially pronounced dead.

It was the eighth drowning along the Grand Strand that summer.

The Surfside drowning took place during the day, while some others have happened after the lifeguards went off duty. A romantic moonlit stroll on the beach, with a quick swim under the starlight, sounds romantic, but it can also be deadly.

Rip currents, or undertow, can flow fast and strong away from the beach, even as waves power ashore. Unseen on the water's surface, this whirling action can sweep away a victim in a few minutes.

Possibly the first recorded drowning at Myrtle Beach occurred on July 29, 1902. A 1970 article in the *Independent Republic of Horry Quarterly* by Lucille Burroughs Godfrey quotes from the *Conway Newspaper:*

"Miss Ruth Burroughs was drowned while out bathing at Myrtle Beach last Tuesday evening, and her remains were not recovered from the waves until about daylight yesterday morning...about three miles up the beach in the direction of Singleton's Swash."

According to the article, a group of fifteen or twenty went out about 7 p.m. to bathe and swim in the surf. The outgoing tide and undertow carried them out farther than they meant to go. Ruth and a Mr. Read were the farthest from the shore. As they recognized their danger, Mr. Read went to Ruth's assistance. She fell unconscious. He fought to keep her head above water, but by now his feet couldn't reach the bottom.

Men on shore launched a boat to help. Mr. Read was almost exhausted when a giant wave tore Ruth from his grasp. He barely escaped drowning himself, while Ruth disappeared.

Ruth's mother, brother, and sisters had left the beach to spend a few days in Hendersonville, North Carolina. Since a friend was coming to visit, Ruth stayed behind.

After the recovery of her body, the little local train, pulled by the wood-burning engine known as the "Black Maria," carried Ruth to Conway. Her family met her there, having made a sad journey by train and carriage. The drowning stunned Conway and the tiny community of Myrtle Beach. Ruth was a happy, fun-loving, Christian girl, who endeared herself to everyone.

From Ruth's drowning until today, the tragedy continues. Most drownings could be avoided by following directions, looking for the lifeguard, and swimming carefully, but the death toll goes on: eight in 1998, five in 1997, two in 1996.

The ocean is a marvelous wonder for waders, swimmers, surfers, and walkers along the beautiful strand. Still the force and power of the current must be respected, or history will continue to repeat itself.

27

HOBCAW BARONY

Waccamaw Neck—what a beautiful place to visit and explore! It comes complete with tales of Indians who roamed the land, and Spaniards who tried to settle in the 1500s, and failed. Pirates often found refuge in coastal inlets and coves. And many notable travelers have made their way along the path called the King's Highway.

Indians called the land *Hobcaw*, which means the "land between the waters." The Neck stretches south from the Horry County line to Winyah Bay, at Georgetown. It extends from the marshes and beaches of the Atlantic Ocean to the dark swirling waters of the Waccamaw River.

In 1718 the Lords Proprietors in England granted Lord John Carteret thousands of acres along Waccamaw Neck. Since he was a nobleman, Carteret's grant was called a "Barony." He soon sold his land, which was divided and sold again to rice planters. Great plantations sprang up. You can still see the boundary ditches between plantations, since fences weren't used. Slaves dug those ditches ten feet wide by ten feet deep. Some of them ran six miles in length.

After the Civil War, rice planting was no longer profitable. The land fell deserted. Here and there, a freed slave who had no place to go might still occupy a hut, but overgrown fields and crumbling mansions became commonplace.

Then came Bernard Baruch.

He was born in Camden, South Carolina in 1870. His father, who had served as a surgeon in the Confederate Army, decided to move his family to New York City in 1880. There young Baruch grew up and graduated from City College.

His first job was on Wall Street, at a salary of three dollars per week. Baruch worked hard and learned all he could. It didn't take long for anyone to see he had talent. He was a millionaire by thirty, and known as "The Wizard of Wall Street." Baruch became one of the richest men on Earth.

For most of his adult life, Baruch willingly served as an unpaid "Advisor to Presidents," beginning with President Woodrow Wilson during World War I. He kept the president so well informed that Wilson nicknamed him "Dr. Facts." Since he didn't work out of an office, others called Baruch "The Park Bench Statesman."

During World War I, Baruch served as Head of the War Industries Board. He acted as an economic advisor at the Paris Peace Conference in 1919. During World War II, Baruch served as Assistant to War Mobilizer James F. Byrnes.

Although Baruch had several homes in the North, he fondly remembered his boyhood days in South Carolina. While on a 1905 hunting trip to Waccamaw Neck, he felt attracted to the tranquil woods, the wildlife, and the beautiful, deserted beach. He deplored the ruin of the abandoned plantations. So Baruch decided to buy property on the Neck.

This portrait of Bernard Baruch
hangs in the Hobcaw House
Courtesy of J. K. Floyd

Within two years he bought eleven of the old rice plantations. Baruch coveted a place of rest and relaxation for himself and his family, and he knew he had found it. When he told friends about his wilderness estate of 17,500 acres and his wonderful hunting experiences, they accused him of exaggerating. Until they came to visit Hobcaw Barony.

The first Baruch house on the Neck burned in 1929. They built their second home to be as fireproof as possible, on a bluff overlooking Winyah Bay, with Georgetown visible across the water. Moss-draped oaks hovered over colorful azaleas, camellias, and native holly and dogwood trees.

Baruch called his nine-bedroom mansion, equipped with every luxury except a telephone, his "hunting lodge." The servants' wing in the back had eight more bedrooms. Baruch didn't want to be disturbed.

In the early days, the family came across from Georgetown by boat. The Lafayette Bridge, completed in 1935, enabled the Baruchs to travel by car along the King's Highway. They loved the view as they crossed the bay: tall, slender white columns gleaming against the rosy brick of the house on the bluff, sheltered by trees and flowering shrubs.

Tennis courts and a playhouse provided fun for the Baruch children. The girls, Belle and Rennie, loved the playhouse, which was equipped with electricity and running water. Bernard, Jr. loved tennis, fishing, and boating.

The family visited their secluded retreat as often as possible. Many friends and well-known persons came by invitation to enjoy the hunting, bird watching, fishing, and the peace and quiet. Visitors included songwriter Irving Berlin, author H. G. Wells, and British Prime Minister Winston Churchill. President Franklin D. Roosevelt came to relax and rest from the strain of World War

II. Pictures and memorabilia in the house tell of these and other visits.

Baruch also bought and developed property between Nesmith and Kingstree, South Carolina, on the Black River. He called this home "Little Hobcaw." After his wife died in 1938, he began to spend the winter months in the smaller house. He loved the quail hunting there. Baruch entertained guests at Little Hobcaw until his death in 1965.

Of the three Baruch children, it was Belle who felt a deep love and commitment to preserve Hobcaw Barony. In 1936 she built her home on the estate and called it "Bellefield." Not only was it named for her, but also for one of the old rice plantations. Then Belle began to acquire other parts of the Barony. By 1956 all of Hobcaw was in her name, as part of her plan, with her father's approval, to preserve the estate.

At Friendfield Village, former slave quarters, Belle enlarged and improved the houses, providing homes for workers until 1952. The village had a small church, and a doctor's office served as a school for White children. Baruch had built a school for Black children in 1915.

Belle strongly encouraged the little ones to attend school, and checked on them often. She loved to fly her small plane, and she often flew over the estate to check on things. Sometimes she spotted children cutting school. When they heard her plane, they tried to hide. She always insisted on the importance of education and proper health care.

Before her untimely death from cancer in 1964, she established the Belle W. Baruch Foundation, a trust fund earmarked for the study of coastal ecosystems. The Foundation's main purpose was "teaching and research in forestry, marine biology, and the care and preservation of flora and fauna in South Carolina." Clemson University and the University of South Carolina maintain research laboratories and educational institutes.

The Hobcaw Barony Visitor Center, operated by the Belle W. Baruch Foundation, stands near the entrance to the refuge. The center, open Monday through Friday, is a small museum with aquariums, terrariums, and a saltwater touch tank, and provides an overview of the research and preservation programs. Audiovisual programs trace the history and development of the estate. A three-hour van tour includes part of the Baruch mansion, the former slave village, and the salt marsh.

Hobcaw Barony, a place of historic beauty, has been preserved through the foresight of a father and daughter who loved the land: Bernard M. and Belle W. Baruch.

Their legacy lives on.

28

BAKER JOHN

"Baker John" Schiller opened his bakery on Ninth Avenue in Myrtle Beach in 1946. The scents of freshly baked bread, buns, rolls, cakes, and cookies drifted through the little seaside town, causing mouths to water and stomachs to growl. Baker John's vibrant personality and sacred conviction to please his customers made him a popular and permanent resident. He had finally come home. His life had always been an adventure.

Schiller was born in 1899 in Vienna, Austria. He grew up in the days of the powerful Austro-Hungarian Empire. The 1914 assassination in Serbia of the visiting heir to the throne caused Austria-Hungary to declare war. Russia mobilized troops. Germany declared war on Russia and its ally, France. Great Britain joined France. World War I had begun. The Ottoman Empire (Turkey) and Bulgaria joined the Central Powers, Germany and Austria-Hungary. Opposing them were more than thirty countries, including in 1917, the United States. The massive loss of life brought about the collapse of the Austro-Hungarian Empire. The Treaty of Versailles changed the borders of Europe and brought about more suffering.

Reduced to a fourth of its former size, Austria offered no hope to its inhabitants. There were no jobs. Food and money were scarce. Many people tried to flee the country. Young Schiller joined a small group who secretly crossed the Alps and ended up in Genoa, Italy.

One night Schiller slipped into the waters of the Ligurian Sea, and swam out to an anchored cargo ship ready to leave for the United States. He silently pulled himself aboard, hid, and sailed as a stowaway. He stayed out of sight until the ship docked in Galveston, Texas to pick up a load of grain. Schiller slipped ashore.

He was twenty-one years old, an illegal alien with no money or papers, and only the clothes on his back. He spoke four languages fluently. Unfortunately, English was not one of them.

Still, Schiller had a dream of what he could accomplish in this great land of America.

He spent his first days looking unsuccessfully for work, and his nights sleeping outdoors in a park. He couldn't sleep well since the police patrolled the park. One night he barely escaped arrest. Schiller was cold and hungry and tired; his American dream seemed far away.

Schiller had been a baker's apprentice back in Vienna, so he finally got a job in a bakery. The owner didn't ask many questions. Schiller worked hard, so the owner let him sleep in a storeroom, on the tops of sacks of flour, until he earned a little money.

Eventually Schiller took the train north to Maryland to find some relatives. They advised him to go to Canada, work a while, and reenter the United States legally. Schiller did. Receiving his citizenship papers was a proud achievement for him, one he cherished the rest of his life.

He moved to Baltimore. With hard work he soon owned three bakeries and eight delivery trucks. All went well until the Great Depression. Schiller sold or leased his bakeries, and went to work as a pastry chef at Johns Hopkins Hospital. There he met his future wife, Ruth, a nurse from Sumter, South Carolina.

After World War II ended, the Schillers decided to move to Myrtle Beach. Ruth thought it would be a nice place to raise a family. Two children, Ruthie and Johnny, were born in Myrtle Beach.

At first Schiller baked fresh bread for Chapin Company Grocery Department Store. He met local people and made contacts. In a short time he was able to open his own bakery on Ninth Avenue North, across from the Methodist church.

In 1946 tourists began to travel to Myrtle Beach to enjoy the beautiful strand. Tires and gas, rationed during the war, were once more available. The King's Highway and a few other roads had been paved. The pavement of Highway 501 to Conway in 1947 brought more vacationers.

Schiller's Bakery was a hit from the beginning. He took orders to local restaurants, hotels and inns, retail customers, and special buyers. If you could describe your cake or cookies, the Schillers could make and decorate them. The whole family worked together.

Baker John particularly enjoyed decorating cookies for special holidays and sharing them with children. He took great trays of cookies to schools and churches as a treat. That way he expressed his gratitude to his great new homeland.

With the expansion of the Pavilion Amusement Park in the 1950s, new rides were added. On one occasion a German-made piece of equipment arrived, complete with installation instructions—in German. None of the workers could read it.

All work stopped until someone shouted, "Go get Baker John! He can help us."

The bakery was less than two blocks away. Baker John soon ran up, wearing a big smile. He translated the German instructions, and the new ride went up.

Schiller retired in 1972 and leased his bakery. After some persuasion, he worked ten more years as pastry chef at the new Hilton Hotel. He retired again at age eighty-three. The Schillers set out to see as much of the country as possible. They drove across the northern states to the West Coast, and returned by the southern route. Schiller loved the country, and made friends everywhere he went. The Hilton Hotels in the towns they visited invited them to stay as guests.

When Schiller and his son made a final trip to Austria to visit family members, they received a big welcome from the huge Hilton Hotel in Vienna. The staff honored them with a great reception.

Baker John died May 26, 1986, at eighty-seven years of age. His funeral service took place at the church across the street from his bakery. Everyone fondly remembered the kind Austrian who risked his life to come to the United States, and made it his beloved country.

29

MYRTLE BEACH AIR FORCE BASE

Late in 1941, rumors of war turned into a real war. The Japanese bombed Pearl Harbor. Then the Germans declared war on the United States, and suddenly enemy submarines lurked in the Atlantic. The battle had arrived at the King's Highway. A base for warplanes was needed.

The years leading up to the war brought changes. The completion of the Intracoastal Waterway in 1936 brought newcomers to the little seaside village of Myrtle Beach. The Civilian Conservation Corps Camp, the opening of Myrtle Beach State Park, and the increase of tourism were only the beginning.

In 1940 the WPA (Works Progress Administration) began work on runways at the tiny Myrtle Beach Municipal Airport, which had been used mainly by owners of small private planes. As the wars in Europe and Asia grew closer, the 3rd Observation Squadron used the runways, and conducted firing practice along the beach.

When the war drew our nation in, the military decided to establish a bombing and gunnery range at Myrtle Beach.

One officer and 188 enlistees arrived in 1942 from Savannah

Army Air Base to organize and operate the new facility. The men lived in tents and huts, with no heating or air conditioning. They worked hard. Buildings went up. Runways grew longer. Planes made regular runs out over the Atlantic.

By 1943 German submarines constantly attacked shipping all along the Grand Strand. Residents welcomed the new air base. The sight and sound of U. S. planes overhead, scanning the ocean, offered a measure of reassurance to nervous civilians.

One incident reflects the attitude of the time. A group of soldiers were one day hard at work on the foundation of a new building. Suddenly came the startling order: "Take cover! Gas attack!"

This was no joking matter. The well-trained men immediately ran for cover and their gas masks. Later they learned what had happened. A shifting wind had brought their way an obnoxious odor, strangely similar to the smell of poisonous gas. To their relief, and chagrin, the odor came from a mill down the coast, south of Myrtle Beach.

Some airmen who trained at the base flew with Lt. Colonel Jimmy Doolittle on the first bombing raid on Tokyo, late in 1942.

On November 8, 1943 the facility officially became Myrtle Beach Army Air Field. It included 100,000 acres of owned and leased land for training, gunnery, and bombing practice.

The beach had become a very different place.

Civilian personnel often worked with soldiers in construction. German POWs moved to the air base. They worked at house-keeping duties or as orderlies in the base hospital. Since Myrtle

Beach State Park was just across the King's Highway from the base, the park was closed to the public and used only by the servicemen and POWs until the end of the war. At first there were few other recreational facilities for the soldiers. There were no cities nearby to visit while on leave. Transportation was a problem. The train went to Conway, then into North Carolina. Bus service was slow and erratic. To some young men who had come from large northern cities, Myrtle Beach seemed like the end of the line.

In July 1943, a service club opened near Withers Swash, not far from the base. Busloads of girls came in to take part in dances. Romances and marriages resulted. A base library opened. The movie in town changed twice a week. In August a bowling alley opened, providing a popular activity for soldiers and civilians.

World War II ended in 1945. Several groups used the base for training and encampment: the Civil Air Patrol, the Air National Guard, and the U. S. Military Academy. Training for the

Troops from the Myrtle Beach Army Air Base parade in 1944
Used by permission of the Horry County Museum

airlift operation for West Berlin took place in 1947. Then in October of that year, orders came to close the base. The army turned the tower and runways over to the municipal airport.

The base reopened in 1953. Colonel Robert Emmons, one of Doolittle's Raiders, became the first commander of what was now called Myrtle Beach Air Force Base. Men and planes left there to participate in the world's emergencies. During the Cuban Missile Crisis, everyone knew the base would be a prime target for a nuclear strike. On October 28, 1962, students and teachers along the King's Highway moved to the inner halls of their buildings and crouched on the floor, as they waited for the two o'clock p.m. deadline that President John F. Kennedy had given the Soviets to begin dismantling the missiles and launchers in Cuba. Also Soviet ships were in route to Cuba with more missiles and equipment. Fortunately the ships turned around and the launchers were dismantled.

Planes and men from Myrtle Beach Air Force Base served in Lebanon, the Dominican Republic, and in Operation Desert Storm, based in Saudi Arabia. The A-10 Thunderbolt II, a ferocious tank killer, earned the distinctive nickname, "the Warthog."

At the height of its operation, the base, home of the 354th Tactical Fighter Wing, had 3,400 active duty members and about 650 civilian employees. It was Horry County's largest employer. In 1991 came the news that the base would close.

The Inactivation Ceremony for the 354th at the Myrtle Beach Air Force Base took place on March 31, 1993. The last notes of

"Taps" had scarcely died away before the skies filled with the roars of the final A-10 flyover, led by Colonel Rick McDow. An era had ended.

One can only wonder if the base might one day again be needed.

30

A SEASON OF STORMS

The word "hurricane" comes from the Spanish word *huracán*, which the Conquistadors picked up from the now extinct Taino Indians of the Greater Antilles and the Bahama Islands of the Caribbean. *Huracán* meant "winds filled with an evil spirit."

Few people will argue with that.

The threat of hurricanes is a fact of life to coastal residents all the way from Brownsville, Texas to Eastport, Maine. Although relatively few strike an area, everyone must always be prepared! Each year brings threats. The season of storms, officially called the "Hurricane Season," begins the first of June and lasts six long months, until November 30th. Severe storms do occur after November 30th, but these aren't hurricanes. They are "Nor'easters," a name borrowed from New England ships' captains in their struggles against the elements. Northeasters' gale force winds barrel down from the frigid North Atlantic.

Myrtle Beach is located on the inland curve of the crescent known as Long Bay. This offers some storm protection. Sometimes the Continental Shelf and the Gulf Stream help turn storms away from the coast toward the northeast.

In earlier times, before weather forecasts, people along the King's Highway studied the skies and wind direction in an attempt to predict storms. Every farm had a weather vane to note wind direction. Residents believed weather proverbs, legends, and superstitions, and often these proved true.

The first recorded Grand Strand hurricane came in 1752. Called a "heavy blow," this storm severely damaged the small, weak settlements of Georgetown and Kingston-on-the-Waccamaw (Conway). Wind and water surge ruined dams and dikes of rice plantations on Waccamaw Neck. It took several years of backbreaking labor to restore the rice fields.

That storm was followed in 1754 by a spectacular eclipse of the sun. It frightened everyone and confirmed a popular opinion that this "haunted coast" wasn't good for settling. In spite of superstition and the threat of storms, the rate of settlement increased between 1753 and 1763.

There have been many recorded "heavy blows" since that first one of 1752. The worst ones are listed by dates in *A Survey History of Horry County, South Carolina*, 1989.

Late in August 1893, the "Great Storm" swept along the beaches, bringing death and destruction. Hundreds of ships sank. Two, the burned hulk of the *Freeda A. Wyley* and the *Jonathan May*, washed ashore at Myrtle Beach. On October 13, 1893, another storm and tidal wave centered on Litchfield Beach and Murrells Inlet. Houses floated away. Residents drowned.

In October 1954, Hurricane Hazel (the witch) had already slammed across Haiti, with terrible destruction and loss of life.

Hurricane Hazel ripped a path of destruction
along the King's Highway, sparing no one.
Used by permission of the Horry County Museum

Back at sea, the storm weakened and crossed Florida, only to turn
back to the Atlantic Ocean and head north. South Carolina
coastal residents rested easy on the night of October 14th. The
witch storm would pass on by, no threat to the Carolinas. Except
Hazel gained amazing strength and made up her capricious mind
to turn toward land. Word of the change in direction went to the
police stations.

Fortunately, the summer tourists were already gone. Still, the
police had to get the word out, and they didn't know which houses
were occupied.

All beaches were going to get hit, but the projected path of
Hazel promised to bring it directly into Ocean Drive, between
Cherry Grove to the north and Windy Hill to the south. Police

Chief Merlin Bellamy rounded up six men. They went out with sirens, lights, and horns to wake and warn people. They knocked on countless doors. Residents hurried from the danger zone.

There's no way to know how many lives Chief Bellamy and his men saved, but save them they did. Hazel timed her visit close to daybreak, at high tide. The heavy, driving rain and 130 mile-per-hour winds created a memorable night and day. Hazel flattened every building in Ocean Drive and Cherry Grove.

About two thousand people took refuge in churches, schools, and other sturdier buildings, while most fled inland. All the beaches suffered tremendous damage. All fishing piers collapsed. Power and water were lost.

Hurricane Hazel went on, strengthening over water, and killing 95 people in New York City.

The silver lining of such storms is the kindness and compassion of people helping others. Myrtle Beach Air Base, Shaw Field, and the National Guard rushed in aid. Rebuilding turned Myrtle Beach into a national resort.

On September 21-22, 1989, Hurricane Hugo struck. Some called it "Son of Hazel." Fishing villages Awendaw and McClellanville, both along the King's Highway, north of Charleston, suffered devastation from the twenty-foot storm surge and the 143 mile-per-hour winds. Then the storm turned north and headed inland. The damage estimates ran to six billion dollars or more.

The naming of storms for women began in 1953, possibly because of the "hur" in the word. In 1979 men's names were added. Hurricanes begin as tropical depressions in warm Atlantic waters near the West Coast of Africa or in the Caribbean. Propelled by tropic trade winds, the depressions intensify as they travel west-northwest. When spiraling winds reach a velocity of 74 miles per hour, the storm is called a hurricane.

From the earliest Colonial days, the threat of storms has been a part of coastal living. It comes with the beauty and mild climate. Residents try to be prepared, and make the best of whatever happens. The only certainty is that another storm will someday strike.

31

GHOSTS OF THE COAST

Some people who have experienced ghostly encounters consider the area around Georgetown, Pawleys Island, and Murrells Inlet one of the most haunted locations on the East Coast of the United States. In fact, Georgetown and nearby areas have the somewhat dubious honor of unofficially being "The Ghost Capital of the South."

Folklore and old wives' tales play an important part in the heritage of the great plantations. Many of the houses in town and on the plantations claim a resident ghost. Any strange sounds or suspicious sights reinforce the rumors. Stories grow with the telling.

Then too, someone said that the coastal area is such a pleasant place to live that even those departed from this life keep coming back.

The Hermitage in Murrells Inlet claims Alice, the ghost of the young lady that searches for her lost ring along the banks of the creek. Many claim to have seen her or felt her presence.

Drunken Jack Island bears the name of an unfortunate pirate

that was left behind by his shipmates. Perhaps he drank himself to death on the tiny island. Does his restless spirit still wait for the pirate ship to return?

Some say Theodosia Burr Alston, lost at sea in 1813 as she tried to visit her father Aaron Burr in New York, still haunts the walkways of Brookgreen Gardens. She longs to rejoin her husband and young son.

The Gray Man of Pawleys Island has warned people of approaching storms since the 1820s. Dr. Tucker still wants to ring the bell at Litchfield Plantation late at night so he can come inside. Some still claim to hear the faint cries of the little boy who drowned years ago while crabbing.

Settlers in the New World brought with them a vocabulary of ghosting. Words like witch, spook, specter, haunt, old hag, and plat eye had special meaning for believers. From England came two names less well known: piskies (pests), and knackers (tricksters). These two are the originators of the trick-or-treat custom.

Ghosts play a part in several primitive religions or cults, among them ancestor worship, witchcraft, and nature worship. Some tribes of Native Americans practiced a "Ghost Dance," in which performers wearing white robes danced on dark nights.

The autumn months are great times for telling ghost stories. There are organized ghost tours, ghost hunts, and ghost walks. Storytellers keep legends alive. Georgetown tours may take you to town houses or country places where the images, noises, or feelings don't always make sense. Dark-o'-the-moon storytelling at Atalaya, the Huntington home in Huntington State Park, attracts big crowds. Old Gunn Church on Plantersville Road draws visitors for its eerie noises.

So the question along the King's Highway, for residents or visitors, is: what should you do if you hear footsteps where no one walks, or see a strange shadow move, or if you get a cold feeling as you pass near a tombstone? From ancient lore and primitive legends comes a fearful warning: "Beware!"

32

THE WITCH'S CURSE

This story doesn't take place along the King's Highway, but it is a legend among the Buck family, who settled Bucksport and Bucksville on the Waccamaw River in Horry County. It involves the head of their clan, Jonathan Buck, of Maine. It's such a good story I had to include it.

Colonel Jonathan Buck was born in Massachusetts in 1719, and heard tales as a small child about the Salem witch trials. In a terror-filled episode of Colonial history, citizens of Salem hanged twenty women as "witches." Two more women died in prison. These stories scared Buck so much that he grew into a strong Methodist, with a Puritanical hatred of witchcraft.

In 1764 Buck moved his family to land he had surveyed along the Penobscot River in Maine. He founded the town of Bucksport, served as Provincial Agent, colonel of militia, and Justice of the Peace. At some point he accused a woman of witchcraft. After her conviction on scanty evidence, citizens of the town prepared to hang her. She pleaded with Colonel Buck to spare her life. He refused. With the woman's last breath, she cursed

Buck and swore to come back from the dead to dance on his grave since he had falsely convicted her. The colonel was a superstitious man, and took the threat seriously.

Some Bucks later headed down the King's Highway to found towns in South Carolina, but Colonel Jonathan Buck stayed in Bucksport, Maine.

The colonel died in 1795, and was buried alongside his wife, who had died six years earlier. Family members erected a fifteen-foot granite marker in his honor.

Not long after his death, the shape of a woman's leg and foot appeared on the marker directly under the name "Buck." The family had the granite sanded and cleaned again and again. The shape stayed. So they replaced the stone with a new one. Soon the shape reappeared. Another new marker was put up. The shape found its way onto it too.

Today the granite marker sits near the road in the Bucksport Cemetery. Crowds come to see the still visible woman's foot.

There are a number of other stories about the foot. And it's certainly not unknown for a flaw in granite to take a recognizable shape. Still, the Buck family monument is considered "one of the most remarkable and curious objects in the state of Maine."

The Buck Monument
Courtesy of the Bucksport, Maine Chamber of Commerce

Courtesy of J. K. Floyd

Blanche W. Floyd was born in Marion, South Carolina and grew up in the Low Country. She has lived in Myrtle Beach since 1950 with her husband, J. K. Floyd. They have three children. Blanche received her Bachelor's Degree from Columbia College, and her Master's Degree from the University of South Carolina. She taught history in Myrtle Beach schools until 1980. She has had numerous articles published in magazines and newspapers, and writes a column for *The Sun News.* Her last book was the popular *Tales along the Grand Strand of South Carolina.*